SKATEBOARD

Parks: Design & Development

Scott Bradstreet

Schiffer Publishing Ltd

4880 Lower Valley Road, Atglen, Pa 19310

Schiffer Books are available at special discounts for bulk purchases for sales promotions or premiums. Special editions, including personalized covers, corporate imprints, and excerpts can be created in large quantities for special needs. For more information contact the publisher:

Published by Schiffer Publishing Ltd.
4880 Lower Valley Road
Atglen, PA 19310
Phone: (610) 593-1777; Fax: (610) 593-2002
E-mail: Info@schifferbooks.com

For the largest selection of fine reference books on this and related subjects, please visit our web site at **www.schifferbooks. com**
We are always looking for people to write books on new and related subjects. If you have an idea for a book please contact us at the above address.

This book may be purchased from the publisher.
Include $5.00 for shipping.
Please try your bookstore first.
You may write for a free catalog.

In Europe, Schiffer books are distributed by
Bushwood Books
6 Marksbury Ave.
Kew Gardens
Surrey TW9 4JF England
Phone: 44 (0) 20 8392 8585; Fax: 44 (0) 20 8392 9876
E-mail: info@bushwoodbooks.co.uk
Website: www.bushwoodbooks.co.uk

Designed by RoS
Type set in Amienne/Aldine 721 BT

ISBN: 978-0-7643-3274-6
Printed in China

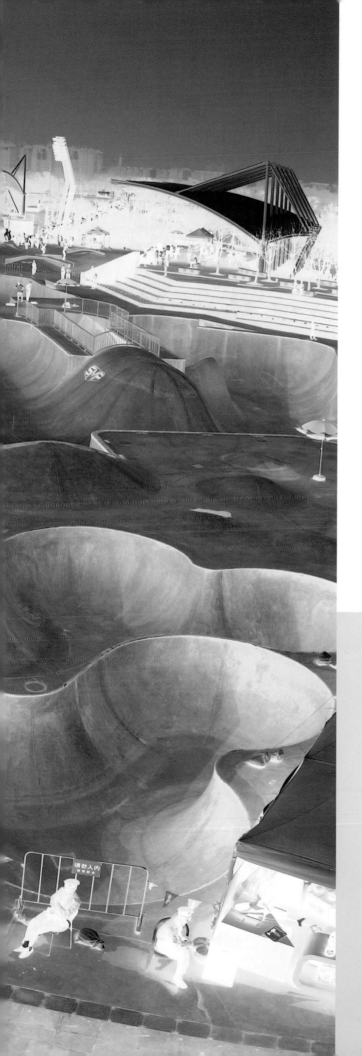

Acknowledgments

People who have made this possible, whether for content or moral support are Jeff Hutchins, John Little, Chris Patnaude, Colby Carter, and Aaron Wallis.

Disclaimer and Acknowledgment

of Trademarks

"If your city doesn't have a skatepark, your city IS a skatepark."

Foreword

This book is written and reviewed by design professionals as a non-biased resource for designers, planners, and governmental agencies. It is not sponsored by or in association with any special interest or advocacy groups.

In the past two decades, skateboarding advocates have seen success in educating the public about skateboarding as it has become a serious recreational activity. With the emergence of role models like Tony Hawk and Shaun White, combined with the popularity of extreme sports, snowboarding, and video games, skateboarding is now recognized by the mainstream as a true sport and not a fad.

Skateboarding facilities are now common to medium and large size cities throughout the United States. They are also expanding and becoming common to the entire world, including countries with large economies like Canada, France, England, Australia, Japan, and China.

Contents

Introduction 7

Chapter 1: History 8

Chapter 2: Regulation 15

Chapter 3: Skateboarding
Facility Types 16

Chapter 4: Facility Elements 26

Chapter 5: Preliminary Planning 58

Chapter 6: Environmental Review
and Processing 66

Chapter 7: Design 70

Chapter 8: Construction 102

Chapter 9: Management and
Operations 120

Glossary 126

A Message from the Author 127

Bibliography 128

Upland Skatepark, Upland, California

Introduction

Purpose of This Book

This book is an education tool for all skatepark development stakeholders: skateboarders, community individuals and leaders, public officials, advocate groups, recreation organizations, design teams, construction teams, and academia. The goal is to provide a comprehensive, non-biased overview of skatepark development. In addition, this book is a fundamental tool for educating those interested in developing their own skateparks.

There are many stakeholders to skateboarding facility development; each is an important piece to the success of a project. However, with so many stakeholders, there are many perspectives, most of which don't ever intersect. The process and past prejudices have crea ed much misinformation and misrepresentation of skateboarding as a sport, of political motivations, and of design authority. Over the past decade, a major effort to educate the public about skateboarding has been made. However, thus far, there has not been an effort t communicate perspectives of all stakeholders as one united front. This book seeks to be the missing link of communication so each stakeholder perspective can be understood and appreciated.

Book Organization

The book you are about to read is organized systematically and somewhat chronologically to make it easy to follow and digest. To understand the roots of skateboarding, this book begins by providing a historical account of skateboarding, followed by a summary of how regulation has impacted this recreation activity turned sport. The reader is then provided an overview of the various skateboarding facility types for a big-picture view, succeeded by a detailed inventory and explanation of the many facility components one might find in a skatepark.

The middle of this book focuses on providing design information to understand the process required to develop a skateboarding facility. This includes preliminary planning, environmental review, and consultant design. This is important in educating design consultants, because they are normally not exposed to the first two pieces of the design process. After summarizing design, this book provides an analysis of the construction methods and procedures to build both the skateable surface and the site development portion of a project. The last chapter of this book reviews the management and operations owners must be prepared to accept when developing a facility.

Chapter 1: History

What is a Skateboarding Facility?

The generic term "skatepark" refers to "a purpose-built recreational environment for skateboarders to ride and develop their technique." (Wikipedia) However, the places where skateboarding occurs and the various equipment skateboarding uses has become so very diverse, that a new phrase is needed. A broader phrase that covers most any facility providing opportunities for skateboarding is, "Skateboarding Facility." We can consider a Skateboarding Facility to be, "any public or private recreational environment with the primary purpose of providing individuals opportunities for participating in the sport of skateboarding."

There are several forms and types of skateboarding facilities, created with various different components. Traditional skateparks are permanent, in-ground concrete facilities, normally featuring bowls and ramps. Newer concepts in skateboarding facilities include skate plazas, street courses, and modular ramp systems on concrete paving. Facilities can be public or private and can be supervised or unsupervised, depending upon admission fee, risk, and security factors.

Skateboarding In the Beginning

Skateboarding as a sport has had almost cyclical growth as it has transitioned from recreation to fad to recognized sport. The manufacture of the skateboard, the opening and closing of public skateparks, and the use of the video camera have all played a role in the development of skateboarding as a sport.

The skateboard originated sometime in the 1950s, so one can consider the sport as originating about the same time. In the 1960s, companies saw the value of the sport and started to produce skateboards. Soon after, skateboarding gained enough popularity that competitions started being held. However, just as it was getting off the ground, in the middle of the decade, skateboarding's popularity died and manufacturers ceased producing boards.

In the early '70s, something huge happened that allowed skateboarding to progress to the next level: the urethane skateboard wheel was created by Frank Nasworthy. This gave renewed interest in skateboarding and manufacturers quickly began to once again produce boards. In the spring of 1975, the Ocean Festival in Del Mar, California, unveiled the true potential of skateboarding as a sport. This is where many saw that skateboarding would be more than just rolling along on a wheeled board, but might also someday involve stunt-like tricks. This and other turns of events induced the opening of several private skateparks. However, once again, skateboarding was just seen as a fad and didn't truly catch on.

The Beginning of Skatepark Development

The genesis of the skatepark was likely an empty pool in someone's backyard with two daring teenagers and a 1950s wooden board with clay or steel wheels. Unchallenged by sidewalks, homemade ramps, and large playground clay piping, but challenged by parents of scarred-plaster pools, skaters created the first skateparks incorporating many of these elements into one. The first concept for a skatepark was a concrete facility with freestyle pads, bowls, and pipes. The crude design of the skateboard in the 1970s limited the ability of the skater and often ended in broken boards when jumps over two feet (not near extreme) were attempted. This also limited the elements that could be incorporated into a skatepark. It was not until skateboards were designed with thick, high-grade plywood, rubber shocks, and polyurethane wheels that extreme jumps and grind obstacles and rails could be attempted.

In the mid-'70s, private owners began to develop skateboarding facilities as for-profit businesses, which lasted about five years. But before skatepark development could really get off the ground, there was a major "skateboarding industry recession." It may have been one or maybe it was a combination of things that caused the recession: economic downturn, growing public liability, or the popularity of roller skating. Whatever the reason or reasons, the recession caused a closure of the majority of skateparks that had been constructed during their decade of growth. Most of those parks developed in the 1970s and '80s were privately built and operated, although some public facilities had existed for a short while.

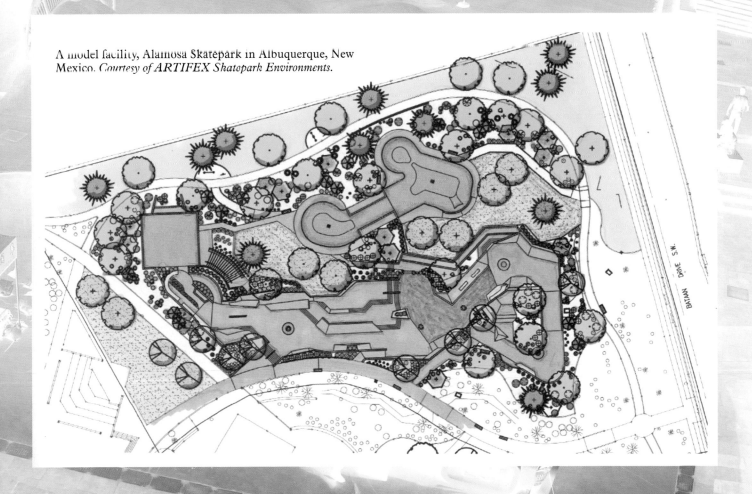

A model facility, Alamosa Skatepark in Albuquerque, New Mexico. *Courtesy of ARTIFEX Skatepark Environments.*

From Skatepark to Vertical to Street Skateboarding

Skateboarding facility development expanded throughout the 1970s, but eventually, interest in developing facilities as a business for profit declined. This era was plagued as demand for land and increase in liability and insurance costs escalated. Skaters were back to creating their own skateboarding facilities in their backyards, schools, and local shopping center parking lots.

Closing of the private skateparks meant that the die-hard skaters had to either construct their own backyard ramps or find other public places. This led to the birth of two diversions from traditional skatepark use: "Vert" or vertical skateboarding and "street" skateboarding in the '80s. Vert skateboarding was an expansion of the use of ramps to allow higher and more extreme tricks. Unfortunately, this new style of skate boarding was definitely a fad style and was short-lived. Once again, a new form of skateboarding could not hold the interest of the fickle skaters and most turned back to the streets.

In 1983, the first "streetstyle" skateboarding contest was held at San Francisco's Golden Gate Park. This event also birthed using video as a media to promote skateboarding. Though vertical skateboarding (on ramps and pipes) grew in the 1980s, it eventually was overshadowed in the early '90s by street skating since there were few places vertical skating could be done (these beginnings later contributed to a rebirth of street skating in the 1980s and eventually the arrival of the Street Course in the late 1990s). As skateboarding at facilities lost popularity in the early '90s, skaters kept the sport alive on city streets. This popularity overflowed from public streets into public spaces, where daredevils pushed the envelope of danger, adding stairways and rails to their typical course of paved streets, walks, and curbs. Though rail skating began in the mid-1980s, it was brought to the forefront with the use of video. Video brought more interest to those who wanted to further challenge themselves (with an element of danger) in the sport. In 1992, Plan B produced "The Questionable Video" with Pat "Handrail Destroyer" Duffy, demonstrating street skating techniques. *Transworld Skateboarding Magazine* declared 1995 the year of the 50-50 grind, and with that handrail skating's popularity soared. From the late 1990s into the 2000s, skating went pro. Rail grinding became so popular that equipment was being manufactured to mimic rails, but in larger and more interesting and challenging forms. The skateboarding market grew so strong that several companies began to manufacture a full line of individual streetcourse elements, not just ramps.

Extreme Skateboarding

In the mid-1990s, the age of technology, the grunge era of music, and the emergence from a recession created the perfect storm for the birth of extreme sports. In 1995, ESPN held their first Extreme Games, where skateboarding was exposed to the mainstream. All of the stunts that had been developed over the years could be performed in public and acknowledged as a legitimate sport. It was at this point that skateboarding would experience importance and never again be seen as a fad. Now, all previous forms of skateboarding: bowls, ramps, vert, and street course were seen as important divisions of the skateboarding sport. Each could be designed as an anchor of a skateboarding facility or could be combined with each other into one facility for a complete experience that would continue to challenge the skater.

The 2008 China Olympic Skatepark. *Courtesy of Convic Skateparks.*

After years of conflict with shopping center owners, police, and parents, an organized movement to educate the public about skateboarding emerged in the mid-1990s. The desire was to create safe, but challenging places for skateboarding that would satisfy all of the stakeholders. It soon became apparent, that for a stand-alone facility to be profitable, it would need to be subsidized by youth organizations or public agencies. A campaign was launched to educate public agencies about the need for skateparks and to develop one in every community.

The first skatepark designed by "modern" standards was Burnside Skatepark, in Portland, Oregon. This skatepark was the result of public pressure to locate skaters in a place away from businesses and public places where they would no longer be nuisances. It was actually built under Burnside Bridge, a location identified as being undesirable for any other types of development. Because of limited funding it was phased through a process of design-build, a method touted by skaters as being the preferred method for skatepark development today. To the City of Portland's amazement, this facility was a resounding success and began the campaign for many cities throughout the western United States (and eventually the entire U.S.) to provide the public with their own facilities.

After about a decade of growth and at the height of development in 2007, it was estimated that over 100 new skateparks were opening every year. Over the last five years, skateboarding as a sport has seen several changes. The growth of skateboarding as a sport has initiated development throughout North America and Europe. An interesting change in the sport is that it used to be a male-dominated sport. Skateboarding is now seeing much more female interest. In addition, the boundaries of innovation continue to be pushed. In the 1990s, street skating meant using existing stairs and rails for grinding. Skaters are now looking to new obstacles, like random banks and oddly shaped structures. As the sport grows and morphs, skaters are always looking for new elements on which to perform their sport. Rock formations, site furnishings, and skateable art are now gaining popularity.

Singapore Skatepark. *Courtesy of Convic Skateparks.*

The Case for Public Skateboarding Facilities

In addition to the simple fact that skateboarders need a facility to perform their sport, there are some good arguments skateboard park advocates use to educate public officials and communities. Probably the most underrated argument made is that, "if your community doesn't have a skatepark, it IS a skatepark." The truth is that skaters want a place to play their sport. Just like children need playgrounds and ballplayers need ball fields, skaters need skateparks. If skateboarders don't have facilities, the result will be undesired skateboarding in schools, parking lots, public parks, and business storefronts. It only hurts the community if the skaters don't have a place to go. Many see displaced skateboarding as vandalism and a nuisance, but it is really just that skaters need a venue for their sport.

Another very legitimate argument made by skaters is that all other sports are provided with facilities for their sport. Shouldn't skateboarders be treated equally? Youth organizations like Little League Youth Baseball and American Youth Soccer Association (AYSO) are provided large, maintenance intensive facilities for use by their organizations, but in communities without skateboarding facilities, skaters have nothing. A good point indeed, because not all children are inclined to or are able to participate in competitive youth athletics. So for the youth who don't participate in competitive athletics, where are they left? Individual sports like skateboarding do not exclude anyone and should be encouraged.

Well-known Skateparks

Within the United States
1. Alamosa Skatepark Environment, Albuquerque, New Mexico
2. Cherry Hill Skatepark, Cherry Hill Township, New Jersey
3. Concrete Wave Country, Nashville, Tennessee
4. The Flow Skatepark, Columbus, Ohio: One of the nation's largest (50,000 s.f.) indoor skateparks.
5. Green Skate Lab, Washington, DC: Features a recycled tire bowl and other recycled elements.
6. Louisville Extreme Park, Louisville, Kentucky
7. Pedlow Skate Park, San Fernando Valley, California
8. Missoula Skatepark, Missoula, Montana: Owned by the Missoula Skatepark Association (MSA), a tax exempt US organization of local skateboarders.
9. FDR Skatepark, Philadelphia, Pennsylvania
10. Rotary Club Skatepark Environment, Black River Falls, Wisconsin
11. Skatopia, near Rutland, Ohio.
12. The No Name Skatepark, Greenville, South Carolina: The second largest indoor skatepark on the East Coast (38,000 s.f.).

Outside the United States

13. The Black Pearl Skate Park, Grand Cayman, Cayman Island: The largest outdoor concrete park in the world.
14. Cairns Skatepark, Australia
15. Emerica Skatepark, Ravensburg, Germany: The biggest outdoor skatepark in Southern Germany.
16. Livingston Skatepark, Scotland: Created by the chairman of the Scottish Skateboard Association.
17. Lota Sk8 Parque, Póvoa de Varzim, Portugal
18. Mei Foo Skatepark, Hong Kong: The largest skatepark in China. SMP Skatepark Shanghai, Shanghai, China: The world's largest permanent skatepark (147,000 square ft.).
19. Paris Skatepark, Paris, Ontario, Canada
20. Shaw Millennium Skatepark, Calgary, Alberta, Canada: One the world's largest outdoor skateparks.
21. Stockwell Skatepark, South London, United Kingdom
22. Unit 23 Skate Park, Dumbarton, Scotland: The largest indoor skate park in the United Kingdom.

The popular indoor facility: Van's Skatepark at the Block in Orange, California.

Chapter 2: Regulation

In the mid-1990s, several design groups led the charge in California to lobby Sacramento to pass legislation that would protect public agencies (municipalities) by limiting the liability for injuries to skateboarders resulting from negligence. Purkiss-Rose Landscape Architects was one of the leaders in this battle. In 1998, California identified skateboarding as an inherently "Hazardous Recreational Activity" (HRA), and thereby limited the liability a municipality would assume for a claim. This allowed municipalities to begin planning for facilities where skateboarding groups pressed for them.

Though this opened the door for skatepark development, insurance agencies were still cautious. They were unconvinced there would be a lessened exposure to liability and thus placed restrictions on policies that dictated skatepark design. A major outcome was that agencies and insurance companies still saw deep bowls not being covered under HRA and therefore created a guideline of a maximum bowl depth of three feet.

There was also some controversy regarding the issue of supervision. Agencies noted that supervision meant a staffing cost, but more importantly meant an acceptance of responsibility for the users of the facility. Therefore, ironically, many agencies that developed skateboarding facilities chose not to supervise them for fear of assuming liability. Instead, when planning the facilities, they have purposely sited them in publicly visual places and even near police stations, so drive-bys become a perceived source of supervision. This doesn't necessarily serve the safety of the skaters, but the safety of the public from the skaters.

In the past decade, with the increased development and success of skateparks, insurance companies have loosened their grip on skatepark design and development. The public education attempts have successfully changed the 3-foot bowl depth restriction so that bowls of 7 to 8 feet are becoming common for new facilities. There are still concerns about supervision, but more sensible solutions are being implemented as skateboarding becomes accepted as a real sport.

So goes California, so goes the nation. Most of the early skateparks appeared in the western United States. Oregon, Arizona, and New Mexico have joined California in the quest to develop skateparks in all large communities. As interest in the sport continues to grow, the standards developed in the west are being implemented throughout the United States and now the world. The United Kingdom and Asia are places where the sport of skateboarding is growing rapidly.

A modern skatepark design at Goodyear Skatepark, Arizona, with deep bowls and some elements that wouldn't have been possible a decade ago. *Courtesy of California Skateparks.*

Chapter 3: Skateboarding Facility Types

With the expansion of skateboarding as a sport, there has also been an evolution of places to skate. Currently, there are over ten different forms or types of skateboarding facilities.

Traditional Skatepark

The most common skateboarding facility is still the traditional, permanent, in-ground concrete facility comprised of at least one bowl. Typically, traditional facilities have a combination of bowls and above ground ramps and elements. "Concrete parks, now 'pretty much the industry standard', according to an editor of *Transworld Skateboarding Magazine*, can cost three times as much to build as parks with ramps and wooden obstacles, but in the long run they require fewer repairs and less maintenance." (Wikipedia)

Goodyear Skatepark in Arizona, a facility with primarily traditional concrete bowls. *Courtesy of California Skateparks.*

Concrete bowls at Chino Skatepark.

Flow Course

A divergence from the traditional skatepark is the "Flow Course," which is designed so skaters can ride a continuous string of elements, normally without large bowls. The advantage of a flow course is its similarity to a racetrack, with traffic flowing in one direction and few intersections. This enables skaters to use more of the facility and reduces the incidences of collisions.

Skate Plaza

A skateboarding facility concept that looks similar to a raised urban plaza, but is designed specifically for skateboarding, is the Skate Plaza. Popularized and promoted by former-professional skater, Rob Dyrdek, this concept usually looks like an elevated concrete performance stage with street obstacles like stairs, rails, and raised planters.

The advantage of developing this type of facility is that it does not require the high costs for excavating and exporting soil to create bowls. Another advantage is there are organizations that offer partnerships for private groups and public agencies who are interested in developing skateparks, but in need of funding. Shoe companies Vans, Nike, and Adidas have the resources and are interested in partnering with others to promote skateboarding. DC Shoes is specifically interested in partnering for the development of skate plazas. They have teamed directly with Rob Dyrdek to develop skate plazas in several locations in the United States. The formation of the Rob Dyrdek/DC Shoes Skate Plaza Foundation has yielded the Kettering Skate Plaza in Rob's hometown of Kettering, Ohio. This 40,000 square foot facility opened in June 2005. Currently, DC Shoes/Rob Dyrdek Foundation is pursuing development of skate plazas in Shreveport, Louisiana, and Cypress, California.

The primary advantage of partnering with a foundation or with organizations is they are willing to partner in the costs of developing the facility, usually willing to cover 50% of the costs. The disadvantage of this is that the agency would have to relinquish some control of construction and operations to the partnering organization. There is also a conflict because partnerships entail the design-build method of development, a method public agencies are very unlikely to use.

Some well-known skate plazas are Highland Skate Plaza in Bellevue, Washington; Stoke Skate Plaza in the UK (the largest in Europe); Downtown Vancouver 'Plaza', Canada; Coeur d'Alene Skatepark, Idaho; Michigan Skateplaza; Henderson County Skatepark; Nevada, Paradise Valley Skate Park; Desert West Skateboard Plaza; Hermoso Park Skate Plaza, California; Milton Keynes Plaza in the UK; Prissick Plaza; and The Plaza at The Forks.

Maloof Money Skate Plaza, Cuperview: a typical rectangular design layout for a skate plaza. *Courtesy of California Skateparks.*

Cairns Skatepark, an angular design that allows a flowing connection between skate elements. *Courtesy of Convic Skateparks.*

Geelong Skate Plaza, an atypical plaza street course with long, straight lanes for continuous skating. *Courtesy of Convic Skateparks.*

Street Course

What can be the least expensive skateboarding facility to develop is the Street Course. A street course can be constructed on a new or existing flat, paved surface. Sometimes street courses are built with some elevation change or as an appendage to a bowl facility. They typically have street obstacles like rails and grind boxes, and sometimes stairs. These facilities might also include skateable site furnishings. In addition to a street course being an inexpensive permanent facility type, the flexibility of design for the obstacles can also make it the easiest to site and develop.

Hollywood Skatepark, a hybrid facility in Clark County, Nevada, with an almost symmetrical layout. Notice the street course elements in the foreground. *Courtesy of California Skateparks.*

Skate Spots

The newest innovation in skateboarding facility developments is the concept of "Skate Spots." These follow a similar concept as "neighborhood pocket parks," where, rather than providing one large community facility, several small skate spots are provided. These serve a greater geographic area within a community and don't require a skater the need to find transportation (like public busing) to visit the facility. A benefit is that skate spots can be located in areas where there are small, unused pockets of land in existing areas where development has already occurred. A disadvantage is that when developing skate spots, there is a possibility of NIMBYs (Not In My Back Yard) not wanting them. Skate spots typically have skate plaza and street course obstacles, but might also have small bowls.

Permanent Wood Construction

The most expensive facility to construct and to maintain is a permanent wood construction facility. This expense is the reason there are few places one can find these facilities. At one time, when lumber was inexpensive, it was feasible to build custom above ground ramps and bowls. In modern times, the cost of lumber makes it impractical to build this type of facility where a concrete facility is an option. Other than a few examples, the only time a wood construction facility is practical, is for professional competitions and Olympic style events. One exception is the Encinitas YMCA, where a custom wood facility is designed and constructed every two years. Since the Y and its skate facility have existed for many years, there is enough popularity and financial support to continue this gem.

Indoor Facilities

One of the types of skateboarding facilities with the most growing interest is the indoor facility. Normally these facilities are located in commercial buildings with concrete floors. The obvious advantage to this type of facility is in programming operations. Indoor facilities can be used in foul weather and at night. A disadvantage can be that, since the facility is enclosed, it always requires on-site supervision. Most of these facilities have modular system components.

An indoor facility, Vans Skate Park at the Block in Orange, California. This facility is nearly all wood, except for a concrete floor and some steel rails and grind edges.

The most flexible concept in skate boarding facilities is a modular system. There are several manufacturers that now produce nearly all of the ramps and street equipment and obstacles in a modular, portable product constructed from wood, masonite, and metal. There are several benefits to having this type of facility. First is that this type of system does not require the cost of hiring a designer. A flat concrete surface is all that is required. Another benefit is the flexibility it provides for the operator. If the operator would like to have a facility with restricted hours of use, this equipment can be stored during off hours. This flexibility also allows the rearranging of equipment and the introduction of new equipment to help keep interest. Modular systems also allow for ease of transitioning between experience levels. Since kids learn quickly, it is good to have some options for expansion. With concrete facilities, what you build is what you get for twenty to thirty years, unless additional land is saved for future phasing or existing features are removed and replaced. Concrete parks are at a permanent risk of obsolescence or failure. Another benefit of modular systems is that they can utilize existing paved areas like basketball and tennis courts to maximize recreation programming. Finally, the ability to move the equipment allows the exchange of new components for dated or worn ones.

There are some disadvantages with modular systems. Though the initial capital outlay for prefabricated modulars is less expensive than concrete, modulars have a five to ten year replacement need, while concrete facilities last for thirty years or more. Over time, modular units deteriorate and exhibit sharp edges, loose screws, and widening lips and joints, which not only are maintenance issues, but can also become safety issues. A concrete park is inherently safer than a deteriorating modular system.

Amazement Park, a modular skatepark built in an unusual location, but with plenty of community interest.

Vert Ramp

The Vert Ramp is a specific type of semi-permanent system. It is a system of large custom ramps, half-pipes, and other vertical structures to perform complicated jumps and aerial tricks. The Vert Ramp was made popular in the 1980s by skaters like Tony Hawk who sought vertical surfaces to do tricks. The Vert Ramp is a wood structure that is usually transported in sections, but it is sometimes constructed on site. It is the predecessor to skateboarding demonstration competitions and extreme skateboarding.

A towering vertical wall at the Olympic facility in China. The 1990s wooden Vert Ramps introduced vertical skateboarding, which has become its own competitive sport. *Courtesy of Convic Skateparks.*

Hybrid

A Hybrid Facility is simply any combination of the facility types. Many modern skatepark designs are now conceived as hybrids, usually with both traditional bowls and street skating elements. It is not uncommon to find a skate plaza with some expanded areas for bowls and pipes.

Combination Use

Some agencies and organizations include BMX, inline skating, and scooters as their user groups. The decreasing popularity and increasing danger of scooters has nearly made them obsolete. Many operators have restricted scooters from their skateparks and have not been met with much resistance. However, inline skating, though decreasing in popularity, is still normally accepted by most operators as an activity that can be done in unison with skateboarding.

BMX as a stunt sport has always been seen as a conflict with skateboarding. This is due to the danger a bicycle can present for skateboarders. In the past, the BMX groups have lobbied for the equal right to use facilities. Agencies have resolved this conflict by providing programming time for BMX when skateboarding is not permitted.

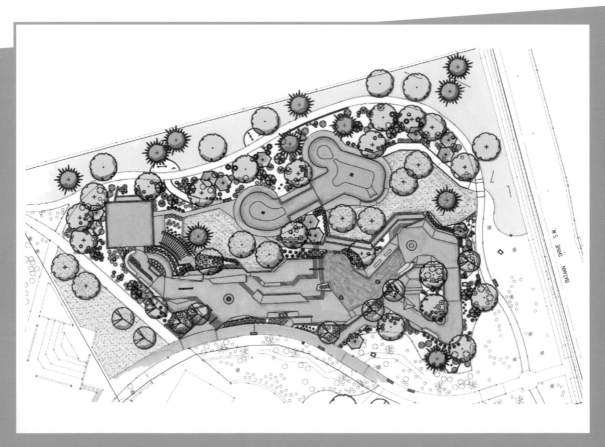

Alamosa Skatepark, a hybrid design with a landscape buffer to separate bowl skating from skate plaza skating. *Courtesy of ARTIFEX.*

A hybrid skatepark in Glendale, Arizona, with mostly bowls, but some added street course elements. *Courtesy of California Skateparks.*

This huge hybrid facility in Singapore was designed to give clear separation of traditional bowls from street course elements with gathering areas and restrooms at the midpoint. *Courtesy of Convic Skateparks.*

Chapter 4: Facility Elements

Also known as obstacles, skateboarding facility elements can be traditional features like bowls, ramps, and pipes. Urban elements like stairs, rails, boxes, and site furnishings are also now commonly designed into most skateparks.

Bowls

Bowls are probably the oldest skatepark components known since they originated as empty swimming pools. Every traditional skatepark has some form of a bowl. Bowls can be a simple half-sphere (a "salad bowl"), but are usually two or more partial-spheres spliced together to create varied and rolling wall surfaces. The most common bowls resemble their prototypes, swimming pools, with three compound half-spheres in one. They also might be in the shape of an oval or a bean.

There has been some controversy regarding the depth of bowls. Some believe bowls greater than 3-feet in depth pose a liability. A 3-feet bowl depth is adequate for beginning skaters, but many intermediate and most advanced skaters prefer the option to challenge themselves with 8-foot or even 12-foot deep bowls.

Because of the practicality of construction and cost, bowls are almost always cast-in-place concrete. However, the Encinitas YMCA has constructed bowls from wood. Wood bowls require high maintenance and because of their proneness to deteriorate, normally don't last much more than a year before replacement is required.

One of the most elaborate combinations of concrete bowls, ribbon curved walls, pipe, and cradles at Lake Cunningham Skatepark in San Jose, California.

Some pool-like concrete bowls at Etnies
Skatepark in Lake Forest, California.

A bowl at Alamosa Skatepark, complete with pool coping. *Courtesy of ARTIFEX*.

Certainly the most common and versatile skatepark obstacle is the ramp. Ramps have evolved over time as the sport has changed. Since ramps can be created by wood or concrete, there are many opportunities to create different shapes and sizes with many results. Ramps, of course, evolved from homemade plywood and 2x4 construction. Some skaters still build their own ramp systems today, probably as a convenience of performing their sport at home. During the 1980s, the Vert ramp was popularized. Today, manufacturers produce commercial grade wood, masonite, and steel ramps that can be transported and stored. Almost every permanent concrete facility also has ramps and in several forms.

A vert ramp is what is used in the XGames and for many demonstrations. It is a large half-pipe (or two, face to face ramps) that has 8-foot or higher vertical walls so skaters can build speed by riding back and forth from ramp to ramp and do tricks as they excel and reach the ends of the vertical walls.

There are actually three purposes for ramps. They can be used to perform turn-arounds, to change direction or to build speed. They can also be used for drop-ins, or they can be used for jumping. Ramps used for jumping are normally concave, but can be sloped. These can be termed, jump ramps, or launch ramps. Concave ramps are also used for drop-ins. Some special forms of ramps can be pyramids (with four sloped sides), spine, and hip ramps (with two sloped sides), and cheek-walled ramps (a ramp sandwiched between two side walls). "Banked ramps" typically refers to sloped ramps. Bank to bank would be two face-to-face banked ramps, similar to a half-pipe.

Small ramps like this one at the Mission Viejo Skatepark are ideal for beginning skaters.

Ramps can
be located
between many
obstacles, like
these well-
used examples
at Etnies.
Large ramps
are used for
building
downhill
speed.

These wooden ramps with no lip at Vans Skatepark are used as primarily drop-ins, but the taller ramp with the steel lip can be used for vertical tricks.

Ramps and banks can sometimes be the same in one, depending on their use. This sloped feature has smooth transitions at top and bottom.

Pipes and Cradles

Pipes are any radiused tube or tube section with no flat riding surface. Pipes are usually found in permanent concrete facilities because of the need for smooth finishes. Smooth surfacing is very difficult to obtain for wood constructed concave surfaces. Though vert ramps are often considered half-pipes, they are not really true pipes because of their vertical walls and flat bottom. Full pipes are complete tubes. True half pipes are tube sections that allow the skater to traverse from side to side. With experience, the side to side traversing can become jumping beyond the ends of the half-pipe to allow airborne tricks. Quarter pipes are long concave walls. There are variations of the quarter-pipe and half-pipe like the mini half-pipe and the super-half-pipe, a mammoth structure for performing extreme sports.

One of the largest and most terrifying full pipes at Upland Skatepark, a 20' diameter concrete tube.

A cradle
at Cairns
Skatepark.
*Courtesy
of Convic
Skateparks.*

An innovative partial pipe design at Alamosa Skatepark. The design creates an "implied" full pipe, but allows natural light to pass through.

Popularized with street course skating and skate plazas, stairs were originally introduced as skate obstacles with the videos of the 1990s. Skating curbs and stairs has become so popular that most every skatepark is now designed with curbs and staircases for the specific purpose of being used as permanent skate obstacles.

Another street course carryover is the wall. All skateparks have walls of varying sizes and shapes, whether straight, stepped, curved, or sloped. Just as every skatepark has walls, most also have "banks" (a sloped plane, less than 100%), which are used where a vertical wall would be a waste of concrete. The advantages banks have as opposed to walls are that they can conform with existing topography, they can act as ramps, and they can be used by skaters for generating speed. Banks are great design elements because they can be designed with many variations, as a flat plane or as concave. For instance, a "taco" bank is a flat plane and transition combined into one.

Concave banked walls at Chino Skatepark.

Straight banked walls at Upland Skatepark that can be used as ramps or drop-ins.

There are many possibilities for stair designs. These examples show integration of stairs with cheek walls and side and center railings.

Walls for skateparks can come in many forms as demonstrated by these examples at Alamosa, Amazement, Rio Bravo, and Cairns skateparks.

Two examples of how street course stairs (Alamosa Skatepark) and walls (Nerang Skatepark) can be fully incorporated into a design.

Cairns Skatepark with banked sidewalls flanking a stairway. *Courtesy of Convic Skateparks.*

Rio Bravo
Skatepark with
an unusual bank
feature that
can double as
a curved grind
wall. *Courtesy
ARTIFEX.*

Pads, Tables, and Ledges

Pads and tables are flat surfaces that are larger than blocks. Though they are similar, their purpose is really to get the skater started, which is why they are sometime called launch pads or manual pads.

A ledge is any vertical drop from a platform into a ramp, bank, or pipe. It is important to distinguish ledges when designing skate facilities because they are needed for skaters to gather speed when approaching other obstacles.

A ledge at Upland Skatepark. Notice there is adequate staging room for other skaters awaiting their turn.

Spines, Saddles, Pyramids, and Pump-humps

An under-appreciated element in skatepark facility design is the spine, a peaked ridged created by the convergence of two opposing ramps. Spines allow grinding on top and can also serve as jump ramps. Saddles are similar, but have radiused or flat tops to create a dual or more gradual edge. A pyramid is a four-sided structure normally with a flat top. It allows skaters to either ride over it or to ride up one side and back down, like a bank. They can also be used as jumps. Pump humps allow skaters to squat up and down to generate energy that is transformed into forward speed.

A spine at Black River Falls. *Courtesy of ARTIFEX.*

This spine at Vans Skatepark is atop a curved bank.

This is a typical concrete pyramid design at Mission Viejo Skatepark.

This prefabricated steel pyramid at Etnies Skatepark also has a spine.

Above:
The convergence of two concave walls form a saddle and with a third end side form a pyramid.

Left:
This custom designed "sculptural pyramid" at Sargent Park and created by ARTIFEX was inspired by a historical skateboarding spot in Europe. It looks like a cross between a pyramid and a spine.

Boxes and Blocks

Boxes became popular with snowboarding, but have become a part of street and plaza skating. One can now find boxes in both permanent and portable skateboarding facilities. There are many names for skateboarding obstacle boxes: fun boxes, grind boxes, bauer boxes, and ollie boxes. Boxes sometimes also incorporate grind rails.

This large wooden monolith at Vans Skatepark incorporates boxes as side-walls to a staircase.

A form that can be considered a block or a table at Black River Falls. *Courtesy of ARTIFEX.*

A series of varying sized and shaped boxes at Chino Skatepark.

Sloped boxes flanking a staircase at Etnies Skatepark.

Rails

As with other elements, there are a number of names to describe the variation of rails; hand rails, grind rails, rail slides, bank rails. Rails, of course, become popular with staircases. The first use of rails was on descending stairways, where a skater could either slide or grind on the top of the rail. The evolution of the rail has produced wide rails for sliding and narrow ones for grinding. The rails might be sloped, elevated, or curved to make for interesting rides. One of the benefit of rails is they are made from steel which can be shaped into many forms like S curves, C curves, and convex curves.

Vans Skatepark has several variations of rails: long, short, level, slightly sloped, and steep sloped.

A parallel set of handrails formed from two different steel tubing types: round and square.

A convex grind rail at Upland Skatepark which allows the skater to ride up and over a pyramid form.

A typical single, round-tubing descending handrail at Chino Skatepark.

There are a number of non-obstacle components every skatepark has to tie all of the obstacles together. To have clear passing and starting space, skateparks need a minimum ten feet of flat bottom between obstacles and opposing transitions. Since skateboarders use flat space to pump and generate speed, maximum flat bottom area allows simultaneous skating without collisions. Especially for flow courses, circulation patterns require consideration of these non-obstacle areas.

When planning for skate component locations, it is important to consider "staging" locations; where the skater is going to drop-in or begin. Raised platforms are the staging areas where the skater gathers initial speed. Platforms are also important to allow viewing of where other skaters are and to avoid collisions.

To tie bowls, ramps, and pipes together, "transitions" are the curved sections connecting two different-sloped surfaces. Transitions for all obstacles need to be fully analyzed. Every transition from horizontal to vertical and to lateral must have either a radiused curve or a banked, tight curve combined with a flat bevel.

Something to consider in the layout of elements is that the most common mistake made in skatepark design is when the designer attempts to satisfy too many needs in a limited space. There must be ample space for passing when riding and for staging when at rest. Many times this is the result of an agency trying to place too many elements in one space because it is going to be the one and only skatepark for the community. If a community is able to design multiple facilities, this can be overcome. A good approach would be to build one primary facility with two or three satellite parks throughout the community.

The urban plaza design for Cairns Skatepark provides clear passing lanes for good circulation. *Courtesy of Convic Skateparks.*

Platforms can come in many shapes and sizes as can be seen by these examples at Chino, Van's, and Etnies skateparks.

With the skating of site furnishings gaining popularity through the magic of videos, urban skating has continued expanding so that manufacturers have been producing skateable site furnishings specifically for skateboarding. Furnishings like benches, tables, and road barriers can now be used as skate elements inside of skateparks instead of in public spaces where this activity would be considered vandalism.

Most skateable site furnishing are now design and fabricated by modular skatepark manufacturers. In this case, Laguna Hills skatepark has an open viewing area so that skaters can actually use the architectural site furnishings as skate surfaces.

Skateable Art

One thing is sure. Skaters are always looking for new opportunities to challenge themselves. After producing site furnishings and seeing their popularity, designers and manufacturers realized there is no limitation to what skaters will use for their sport. Designers are now creating "skateable art." Skateable art can be just about anything: rocks, sculptures, colored surfacing, and other features that are built-ins.

ARTIFEX Skatepark Environments design Alamosa Skatepark with rocks and boulders for skateable art. The boulders create a rare challenging obstacle for skilled skaters.

This skateable art at Geelong Skatepark, designed by Convic Skateparks, provides an almost deconstructionist appeal.

Chapter 5: Preliminary Planning

Budgeting

Experts recommend the average skatepark be planned to be 10,000 to 15,000 square feet (or ¼-acre). A full-service skatepark designed to meet all skill levels will be between 18,000 and 25,000 square feet, with 10,000 square feet being the minimum. This is the area needed to design a facility that separates beginner and intermediate/advanced areas. According to industry experts, whether intermediate/advanced areas are provided, all parks should have beginner areas "between 5,000 to 8,000 square feet and should have slow sloping areas with small hips, moguls, banks, curbs, and rail slides that range in height from eight inches to four feet." A distinction should be made that this includes only the skateable surface and not the supporting site development.

Depending upon the type and size of the facility, it can cost anywhere between $25,000 to $1 million to develop a $10,000 s.f. skateboarding facility. An article in *Landscape Architecture Magazine* cites the Skatepark Association of the U.S.A. as indicating, "a rough cost estimate for a 10,000 square-foot facility can vary from $25,000 for a portable or wood ramp park to $200,000 for an in-ground concrete park, and the cost per square foot can range from $10 to $20 or more. Costs for steel-frame modular parks usually fall somewhere between those figures, with a 10,000-square-foot park starting at around $30,000." (Sunday, 16 September 2007, "Building a Skatepark: Modular or Concrete," by Carol Newman, *Landscape Architecture Magazine*) Once again, it is important to know that this is only the skateable part of the park. In reality, other costs like land acquisition, design fees, site development, environmental review, document processing, and construction management and inspection fees (soft costs) can quintuple the construction costs. "Most concrete skateparks will cost between 20 and 25 dollars (USD) per square foot to build ($270 USD per meter)" for the skateable surface. It is claimed that parks worth building, (those with site development and soft costs) are a minimum of $250,000 to fund (Skaters for Public Skateparks).

My park planning and budgeting experience for recreation facilities has helped to understand all of the hard and soft costs associated with development The most expensive facility is going to be a permanent concrete facility requiring the purchase of land, hiring of design consultants, inclusion of buildings and site development components (grading, utilities, parking, walkway, landscape, lighting), proper processing and construction management, and, of course, construction of the actual in-ground skateboarding facility components. For a full-service hybrid facility, a total project budget might also include site furnishings, vending machines, start-up costs, and FF&E (fixtures, furnishings, & equipment), like lockers and security cameras.

All costs considered, a modern hybrid skateboarding facility, complete with proper design, restrooms, utilities, beginner, intermediate, and advanced areas, multiple bowls, and street course or skate plaza elements is going to be around $1.5 million. Beginner only facilities with all the site development features will cost about $500,000. One of the big costs is a restroom building and its supporting utilities. This can easily add $150,000 for a pre-fabricated or $500,000 for a constructed-on-site building. That is why agencies are tentative about installing restrooms up front. In contrast, skate spots without restrooms and all the other accoutrements can cost as little as $50,000. For the owners without funding sources, the least expensive, but sizeable, skateboarding facility is going to be a modular system placed on an existing concrete slab that is currently owned by the agency or developer.

If a project does not include site development and soft costs in its total development budget, the project manager will certainly be seen as allowing "scope creep." This is not the way to gain support from the political and financial stakeholders and not the way to establish a sense of trust for the sport of skateboarding in general. It is essential for the credibility of both the project and the skateboarding community that costs are accurately estimated and reported.

BLACK RIVER FALLS SKATE PARK

SCALE: 1"=16'-0"

Preliminary budgeting is important to establish a baseline. After establishing the baseline budget, it must be continuously updated during the design of a project. It is wise to prepare a cost estimate at the conceptual design stage and at the construction document phase. If this isn't established at the beginning, a project will be delayed, phased, or tainted by controversy. Shown here is a conceptual design drawing used for estimating a preliminary budget.

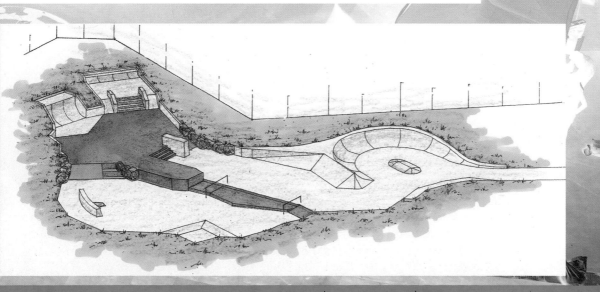

Most people don't oppose skatepark development. However the stigma that comes with skateparks has caused advocacy groups to want to educate the public and public agencies. Occasionally this effort has led to success, but usually not. It often turns off the agency where the development is proposed. The problem with this approach is TRUST. Trust is earned in a relationship when one side is given a small amount of responsibility and acts responsibly. The trust grows with expanded responsibility until complete trust is built. Trust in not earned by organizing into a large group and telling others they need to be properly educated about something of which they are ignorant.

An approach more likely to meet with success is to empathize with the governmental agency. Realistically, elected officials have limited time and control to learn the details of skateboarding or anything else with which they are unfamiliar. They must make big-picture executive decisions with summary information. Elected officials really only have a two-year cycle in which they can affect change. If they can't be fully educated in that short amount of time on a subject they likely have little knowledge (and possibly little interest), there is questionable chance of success. Many citizens and special interest groups don't understand that a five or seven-member city council or supervisory district can change direction every two years as new members or supervisors are elected. One vote in five or seven can easily change the total vote and power of the decision-makers. For this reason, it is important to start implementing a public education effort soon after an election and not six months before.

There are very fundamental differences between private and public development. Private developers and the general public at large are often unaware of the intensive process of public policy. Public officials and employees do not especially like the bureaucracy in which they function, but understand why it is in place. Public employees are also to be objective and not be advocates of projects, but presenters of unbiased information. The policies and processes in government were put in place to protect the people and to allow every citizen the opportunity to be heard. To execute this, everything done must stand the test of time. With good policy, extensive efforts are made to establish public record documents that are historically, factually, and grammatically accurate. Facilities designed and constructed are projected to last fifty years and to serve the maximum number of citizen groups over that period. Budgets are prepared with long-term planning, often forecasted five to ten years into the future. Since public agencies are required to enforce the law, they are also compelled to obey it, and thus perform very rigorous environmental review for their own projects. Projects are also subject to the public works contracting code, which means they must be constructed with prevailing wage labor, even though the contract is awarded to the lowest responsible bidder. All of these factors make the public process very tedious and often very unrewarding. Considering the bureaucracy of the public process, skatepark advocates should empathize with public officials and understand why they have limited time to be educated on something new (or perceived as new).

If skatepark advocates want to be heard, it is not a matter of forcing others to listen, it is a matter of earning trust. The best approach is to become a community advocate first. There are a number of ways this can be done, but they all start with the same path: volunteer work. Most cities have many volunteer commissions, committees, and opportunities. Large cities even employ volunteer recruiters to help plug individuals into the right opportunity. Skateboarding advocates can serve on Parks and Recreation Commissions. This is not a new concept. Many Parks and Recreation Commissioners are also Little League coaches and advocates, which is why they are able to give a voice and implement their organization's needs. Cities also have committees for short-term volunteer work. Events committees for annual holidays, celebrations, Earth Day, and community activities have many opportunities for volunteer service. One of the oldest youth organizations, the Boy Scouts, requires volunteer work to earn Eagle badges. Many Eagle Scouts volunteer for city projects building trails, cleaning litter, and various other projects. In addition, high schools and college entry boards are now requiring students to perform community service for educational credit or admission requirements. This is also one of the executive branch's new proposed national policies for the United States in 2009.

Probably the best ways for skatepark advocates to gain attention is to organize and identify individuals to assist in a number of volunteer opportunities. Adults can volunteer to participate on the Parks and Recreation Commission and children (under adult supervision) can participate by cleaning trash or graffiti at a park or public facility. This will gain the attention and the trust of the city where the facility is desired, because they will know the users of the facility have taken pride and ownership of it.

Depending on the owner and level of supervision for a skateboarding facility, insurance requirements can actually influence the design. Many public agencies are cautious about developing facilities that could have perceived high liability. Though current regulation protects public agencies, many of them are still resistant to designing deep bowls and advanced and expert elements. Most public agencies will not supervise their facilities because they perceive the risk of liability to be higher. It is the quasi-public and non-profit operated facilities that are more likely to have supervision and advanced skate elements.

Depth of bowls and supervision are the two biggest factors public agency risk managers consider in the development of a skateboarding facility.

Stigmas

The stigma that has long plagued the image of skateboarding has come from legitimate concerns. The stereotype of skateboarders being renegade vandals grew from the skaters who created the street courses on public streets. The fact that skateboarding is an individual sport and not a team sport has also created an image of non-conformist, non-teamwork-oriented individuals. Whether justified or not, this image has damaged the sport for those who play by the rules. Contrary to the stigma, skateboarding can actually be a family sport and one that does not discriminate in strength, body size, or class as many other sports do. It is important to understand the history of stigmas in skateboarding when considering developing a facility. One must be prepared to calmly answer the concerns of those who are against skateboarding, stay focused on the goal, and not get offended.

Stakeholders: Users, Special Interests, Agency Officials, and Citizens

Whether admitted or not, everyone in a community with a skatepark is a stakeholder. It is absolutely imperative that everyone with a voice in a community be heard before the project is developed. If not, their voices will be heard after and will cause problems. Skateboarders must be heard because they will determine whether or not a facility is a success functionally. If they are unhappy with the process or the product, it will become public knowledge in schools, adjacent communities, and on the Internet. If skaters are unhappy and the special interest groups learn, they will support the skaters and put pressure on public officials and the community.

In addition to satisfying the skaters, if citizen's voices are not also heard, they can create problems for public officials and put pressure to restrict use or even shut down a facility.

With all this potential controversy, it would appear the best solution would be to not build a facility or to build a minimalist facility that just appeases the users. However, this rally just creates a short-term answer, which just defers the final solution. Many agencies are seeing the benefits of bringing people together to also work together in creating a place where members of the community can gather. This is how community members learn to take ownership and how unity is built.

Development Management Strategy

There are three phases in the development process and three possible strategies for approaching development. The phases are planning, design, and constructions. The management approaches are management by owner, owner's representative, or design consultant.

If the owner chooses to guide the process, he accepts the risk and responsibility for the development. This approach may save costs up front and provide perceived control, but it is shortsighted.

The second approach is for the owner to hire an owner's representative, like a construction manager, engineer, landscape architect, or skatepark designer. This will assure consistency over the project from beginning to end and will direct the responsibility to another party. Most landscape architects are familiar with the development and public workshop processes.

The last approach is to hire a designer (construction manager, engineer, landscape architect, or skatepark designer) for the planning process and if the relationship is to continue, extend the contract through the design process and into construction administration. If the designer is a design-build skatepark consultant, it is unlikely a public sector contractual relationship would be able to continue through the construction process, unless as an independent construction management consultant overseeing the second party (the construction contractor). This is because public agencies find the oversight and construction by the same firm a conflict of interest and don't typically contract design-build services.

Project Definition

Site Analysis

Construction Phase Services

Most landscape architects and skatepark design consultants are familiar with the process required for the design phase of the development process. In most cases, the owner or owner's representative would need to facilitate the planning phase and then hire the design consultant. Shown here are the steps a design consultant uses through both the design and construction phases. *Courtesy of ARTIFEX*

Local Inspiration

Community Involvement

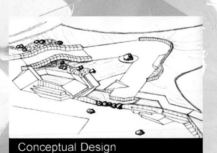

Conceptual Design

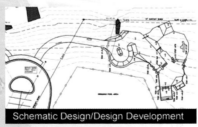

Schematic Design/Design Development

3D Visualization

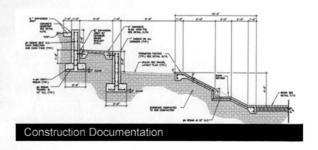

Construction Documentation

Public Process

The most important piece of preparation for development of a skateboarding facility is the public process. When a skatepark comes to a community, it has to be properly received by the community to be a success. Public meetings will be required in the initial planning to develop a relationship and good record with the community. There will also need to be public workshops during the design process where stakeholders are invited to provide input. This gives the opportunity for everyone to take ownership of the facility.

Facility Size

When planning for a skateboarding facility it is important to know exactly what size the facility is to be. When designing a facility, oftentimes sites are selected that are the size of the skateable surface. However, it is important to remember skate facilities need parking, restrooms, spectator areas, and landscape. For a rule of thumb, a site needs to be at least double the size of the skateable surface. In fact, sites are often three times the skateable surface when including parking. The average size skatepark without parking is half an acre, one acre with parking. A two-acre site would be considered large and is sufficient for site development and parking. Keep in mind, the site for a skate spot only needs about a ¼-acre area since they are usually parked on public streets.

Site Elimination

In planning for a public skatepark, there are many factors to be considered in selecting the optimum site. The site must present minimal impact to the community. Factors like visibility, safety, noise, loitering, and pedestrian traffic impact site selection from the community's perspective. From the skater's perspective, site selection factors can be proximity to bus routes, schools, and parks. Since skateboarding doesn't require special site consideration, facilities can be located in "non-desirable" areas. Burnside Skatepark in Portland, Oregon, is located under a highway bridge, where noise and visual impacts are not a factor. Etnies Skatepark in Lake Forest, California, is located next to a highway and in an industrial park complex, where it has little impact on residential areas, because there are none surrounding it. Because of concerns with monitoring usage, many public agencies locate their skateparks in highly visible locations along major streets or adjacent to police stations.

The First Skatepark Master Plan

Most cities and counties have park master plans for planning all of their recreation facilities. These assist in the development process by prioritizing capital projects based on the needs of the community. They establish the requirements for open space acreage and the distribution throughout the community.

As skateparks become more prevalent, agency recreation departments are gaining acceptance and implementing proactive planning. The City of Portland, Oregon, was the first city to approve a comprehensive master plan for skateboard park development. On August 3, 2005, the Portland City Council approved a plan recommending development of 19 skateparks: 13 neighborhood skate spots, 5 district-wide skateparks, and one central community skatepark.

As planned developments continue to flourish, there is more likelihood that skateparks will be planned as planning for ball fields, pools, and passive parks occurs. With the advent of the skate spot, it is now possible to utilize small undesirable acreage, where at one time, that acreage had no use. It will be interesting to see if, in the future, this becomes more common. At minimum, we can definitely expect to see new cities with proactive general planning that includes a community skatepark as a recreation facility.

Following preliminary planning for developing a skateboarding facility, an environmental impact report (EIR) is normally implemented. Just about any jurisdiction is going to require an EIR. Once considered the tool for assessing the negative impacts on the natural environment, EIRs now include nearly anything that will change as a result of the proposed development like lighting, noise, air, parking, traffic, visuals, and storm water.

Lighting

As with ball fields, skateparks with night lighting can change the local skyline. Depending on the hours of operation, overflow of lighting can be an impact for the local stakeholders. The latest innovations in sports lighting allow overflow to be controlled. However, to be sure that there will be proper operations controls and minimal overflow, there will most likely be a need for a lighting photometrics study to be performed.

Noise

Probably the biggest factor in assessing the negative impacts of skatepark development is noise. It is usually best to find a site near an existing busy street or a highway, where noise already exists. The noise generated by a skatepark makes it a poor candidate for residential areas.

Air Quality

It is unlikely a skatepark would have a negative impact on air quality, but if public smoking is permitted, there could be a need for concern.

Parking

Though community parks usually require the most parking, and skaters are not likely to drive to their destinations, parking is a factor in developing a skatepark. Parking ratios are likely half of what they would be for ball fields and typical park amenities. City planners might be willing to consider on-street parking as an alternative to constructing large parking lots that don't really get used.

If a facility is to be operated at night, it will have lighting. These tall sports lights at Chino Skatepark show how lighting can have the potential for an adverse visual impact on adjacent residential development. This skatepark is actually located within Ayala Community Park, so it does not impact the residential neighborhoods.

The noise a skatepark can generate can be a problem in a residential area or in a business district. Amazement Park was located at a former train depot and Etnies Skatepark was planned adjacent to a major highway so the noise they generate is actually minimal compared to the existing noise elements in the vicinity. Courtesy of ARTIFEX.

Traffic

The vehicular traffic generated by skateparks is minimal compared to other community park facilities. One thing that does need to be considered is the creation of adequate drop-off areas. In most cases, an on-site drop-off will be needed to eliminate drop-off congestion on public streets.

Visual Impacts

Though the tricks performed at skateparks can be quite visually appealing, the general public at large would consider skateparks visual blight. This would typically be the second biggest factor in an environmental assessment. The easiest solution is to provide screen walls. However, there is a double-edged sword with this issue because, where walls and landscape are to be used for screening, visibility for security is obstructed. A compromise might be to provide a "filtered" screen with partial open fencing or landscape.

Storm Water Pollution

As with air pollution, storm water pollution in skateparks is normally not going to be a factor. In fact, with some innovation, there can be opportunities for on-site storage and treatment of storm water.

One of the benefits of designing skateparks is that they normally don't have impacts on storm water pollution. Though concrete surfacing increases the potential for run-off, drainage can easily be captured for filtration on-site. This can be a positive in locating a facility near a water body as seen at Cairns Skatepark. *Courtesy of Convic Skateparks.*

Concerned with disturbing the surrounding mountain views, ARTIFEX Skateparks designed the Rio Bravo Skatepark to mimic and blend with not just the materials of the mountains, but even the forms.

A parking drop-off at Etnies Skatepark.

Etnies Skatepark is located in an industrial and commercial area, with clear distances and landscape buffers.

Alamosa Skatepark was constructed adjacent to the public library, which means it had to integrate with the surrounding community facilities. This was achieved using natural materials and a visually appealing architectural design.

The Design Team

There are two components to the design of skateboarding facility: the skateable area and the site development. It is very important to know this for the success of all the users. Both parts require a design specialist with his or her own set of skills. Because of this, it is crucial that two design specialists team together to conceive the synergy for the best outcome. The skatepark designer is the specialist responsible for designing within the skateable area and the landscape architect is responsible for the site development. There has been some disagreement about who is the better designer and who is more qualified to design skateboarding facilities, but the reality is BOTH are needed for the design and needed for each other. The tricky part is that it is always best for the skatepark designer to perform design-build, but the landscape architect only designs and does not construct projects. There are new design firms emerging now that have realized the benefit of having professional skateboarders, skatepark designers, and landscape architects under one roof. This appears to be the future of skateboarding facility design.

Design Methods

Design-build

It is extremely difficult to achieve the precision required for safe, skateable surfaces without having control over construction. That is why "design-build" is the most preferred method used by skatepark designers. Design-build is the method by which a prime entity is responsible for both designing and constructing a project. In the world of construction, the design-build method is used for developing projects from large buildings to small improvements that are "turn-key." Turn-key projects are those where the owner invests the capital costs and is delivered a final product that is ready to occupy as soon as the owner turns the key of the front door for the first time. With design-build, the general contractor is almost always the party responsible for overseeing the project. The general contractor not only hires the subcontractors, but also the entire design team.

One of the advantages of design-build is that the owner has better control over the project because he has one leader in charge of the entire project and with whom he must interact. This allows the owner more freedom to spend time on additional projects or activities. Another advantage is the control of schedules. Since the design team is contracted directly with the general contractor, the general contractor is able to coordinate directly with the design team for processing plans and during construction operations. This makes for better communication. For skatepark construction, design-build means more control over construction precision. It is very important that the riding surface be smooth and clean. It is also important to have flexibility of making field changes in case what was on paper does not get constructed properly in the field. When the same party designs and constructs the project, they have more knowledge and more hands on experience with the project. They are also not going to blame the designer for mistakes.

One of the disadvantages to design-build is that the owner must entrust all responsibility to one general contractor. If the owner is not satisfied with the one general contractor, it means the entire development team could be disrupted, where as the traditional design and construction approach, the owner may directly interact with, and replace any of the development team members at his discretion. Probably the biggest problem with the design-build approach is regarding public projects. It is often misunderstood by design-build companies that cities don't want to design-build their projects. The reality is that because of public contracting law, public agencies have two different criteria for letting contracts: proposals for designers and bids for contractors. The public contracting law requires that, for large projects, contracts be open bid to the entire public and that the lowest qualified bid be accepted. However, for design services, public agencies have a different set of rules. They must solicit proposals and select design consultants, without considering cost. The consultant is selected based upon their qualifications and not their fee. Once the most qualified consultant for the project is identified, the fee is negotiated. If a reasonable fee cannot be negotiated, the next qualified consultant is selected. Since these two methods of selection are not the same, public agencies are usually resistant to hiring design-build firms for their projects. One way to avoid this conflicting criteria is to pre-qualify firms. However, this method is very time intensive and is subject to the city attorney's approval. To sum it up, the design-build approach is not a method most public agencies are willing to use because of the complications. They are much more likely to conform with the traditional approach to designing and constructing a skateboarding facility in two separate contracts.

Private developers are not subject to the public contracting code and can, therefore, freely use the design-build approach for their projects. The problem with this, however, is that there are few developers interested in building skateparks because, as with most recreation facilities, skateparks are not typically a profitable venture. Usually, private development is backed by a foundation or other entity. These ventures must also include a strategy for operations, something else public skateparks are more likely to be able to achieve.

Alamosa Skatepark, a design with colorful materials and unusual forms.
Courtesy of ARTIFEX.

The Traditional Approach

The traditional approach is to design a project first and then build it. Public agencies are able to conform to the public contacting law with this method. Currently, it normally takes a public agency at least two years to design and entitle a skateboarding facility. A public agency hires the design consultant by requesting proposals from consultants. The consultant designs the project and then the agency conducts the entitlement and environmental review process. When the schematic design plans and documents are approved, the construction plans are completed, and then the project is advertised for public bid. The contractor awarded the project is the lowest cost, but qualified bidder.

The primary advantage to the traditional approach for public agencies is that it allows them to avoid the entanglements of the design-build approach. It also allows agencies the flexibility of design changes and phasing or to delay the project. A city can design the project and then wait until capital funds are available to bid it. Probably the biggest reason public agencies would advocate the traditional approach is because it allows ample opportunity for public and environmental review. The last thing a city wants is for a project to hurry through development and be constructed, only to be closed because complete environmental review was not satisfied and the NIMBYS have appeared.

Design and Development Process

There are varying perspectives regarding the design process for skateboarding facility development. Most experienced skatepark design and landscape architecture firms have a truncated view of the entire process from beginning to end. In reality, when developing a public project, there are many complex steps that must be followed to ensure complete involvement of all stakeholders and to achieve conformance with the public contracting code. A public agency's process would look something like the following.

PRE-DESIGN PHASE
- Budget Preparation
- Council Authorization to Request for Proposals
- Consultant Short-listing
- Consultant Interviews
- Consultant Selection
- Award of Contract

SCHEMATIC DESIGN PHASE
- Design Team Kick-off
- Public Workshop
- Master Plan Preparation
- Site Analysis and Selection
- Feasibility Study
- Land Acquisition
- Schematic Design
- Environmental Review
- Management and Operations Planning
- Planning Approval

DESIGN DEVELOPMENT PHASE
- Design Team Meeting
- Public Workshop
- Design Development
- Cost Estimation

CONSTRUCTION DOCUMENT PHASE
- Construction Document Preparation
- Structural Engineering
- Construction Management Services Selection
- Authorization to Advertise for Bids

BID PHASE
- Bidding
- Contractor Selection
- Award of Construction Contract
- Award of Construction Management Services Contract

CONSTRUCTION PHASE
- Ground-breaking Ceremony
- Pre-construction Meeting
- Construction

OPERATIONS PHASE
- Post-construction Activities
- Grand Opening
- Occupation
- Maintenance and Operations
- Future Phasing

Site Selection

At the start of the project, a list of all potential sites will be generated. Through the environmental review process, the sites NOT in consideration for development will be eliminated from the list. It is likely the environmental review phase will eliminate sites near residential development, private businesses, and senior centers. The list of potential sites at this point will now include a number of sites where development IS acceptable. During the design phase, the sites will be prioritized so that the best site can be selected. Criteria for selection might include proximately to freeways, streets, schools, parks, bus routes, and neighborhoods with skaters. Other factors that would help prioritize sites might be site size, value of land, lighting, security, visibility and site orientation, and topography.

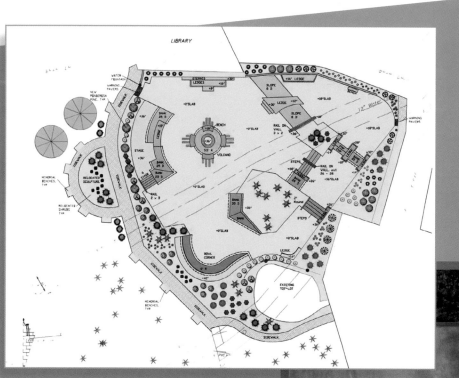

The conceptual plan for Alamosa Skatepark. *Courtesy of ARTIFEX.*

User Demographic Considerations

When designing a skateboarding facility it is important to know the demographics of those who will be using the facility. It is important to assess the level of expertise of those who will be using the facility. If the facility is located in a neighborhood with new development and young families, the skatepark should be designed for beginning users and up. If a facility is being developed in an existing community with a large teenage population, like Etnies, Lake Forest, it is going to serve advanced skaters. It is probable that parking quantities are going to be higher with beginner facilities, because young children are more likely to be driven to a facility and less likely to ride to or take a bus to a facility. When designing a facility, it is important to remember everyone who visits the facility: multiple user groups and those who won't actually be skating. If there are going to be large groups of individuals like kids' camps, the facility will need to include seating areas to serve these groups. If recreation events like skateboarding competitions, musical entertainment, or celebrations are to be a part of the development, areas will need to be dedicated for staging and eating. Also important is the possibility that families might use a facility. If there are going to be younger siblings at a skatepark, they will need safe locations (probably fenced) and their own activities. Younger children might have flat areas to learn skateboarding or they might have playground equipment. There would also need to be seating and viewing areas for parents.

Skateable Area

The skateable area is the portion of the site that is often design-built by the skatepark designer. It is a specialized design that is only made possible by someone with expert experience in skateboarding and at least average knowledge of construction. Often the skatepark designer

employs a team of drafting technicians and 3D modelers who can capture the vision for the skatepark. During construction, the skatepark designer also directs a crew of skilled craftsman who construct and shape that vision in the field. Since public agencies normally don't contract design-build, they will hire a design-build skatepark firm to design a facility. They will then publicly bid the project and hire a different design-build firm to construct it. Then, to ensure quality control and that the originally intended vision is reached, they will also hire the first design-build firm to oversee and construction manage the actual building of the facility. This process may seem to be overkill, but it is needed to conform to the public contracting code and to achieve the best quality.

Some bowls and skaters at Etnies Skatepark.

Site Design Layout

Working with the skatepark designer, it is the responsibility of the landscape architect to plan the overall skateboarding facility layout. Together they use bubble diagrams to determine the gross locations for skateable area, buildings, parking, group use areas, and site elements.

Parking

Most public agencies have parking requirements for private development, but few have defined requirements for public parks and specifically for skateboard parks. It is difficult to calculate parking ratios for skateparks because there are so many variables like quantity of elements, off street parking, walk-to (ride-to) use, and multiple recreation use. In general, skateboarding facilities don't require the quantity of parking sports fields and courts do. However, they DO require large drop-off areas. Drop-offs need to have warning paving strips so skaters know when they are entering vehicular areas. It is common to see zero-curb (flush) paving with bollards at drop off zones. Driveways and aisles in parking lots need to have rough-finished enhanced paving and traffic calming measures to slow both skaters and cars.

Group Use Areas

If special events are planned for skateboarding facilities, large group use areas need to be included in the design. The City of Carlsbad holds an annual "Amps and Ramps" event, where bands and skaters compete at the same time. A temporary stage is placed at the Carlsbad Skatepark for a "Battle of the Bands" while skaters perform their skills. Other events, like birthday parties and youth camps, require large gathering areas, which can be open turf seating areas, amphitheaters, or shaded picnic areas.

Variations of textures and colors for a parking paving at a drop-off zone in front of Etnies Skatepark.

It is important to plan for group use areas and viewing areas when designing. These examples at Etnies, China, and Upland skateparks show some different approaches to designing with turf and seating.

Other than community buildings, there are basically two buildings that could appear at a skateboarding facility: concessions and restrooms. The primary concern with concessions is the operations. It is speculative whether it benefits a public agency to run a food service operation because of the need for a food and beverage license and for staffing the facility. It is more likely a private organization would have concessions. However, like with Little League Baseball, there can be non-profit organizations that could operate a facility if a city is willing to build it.

The other building found at most skateparks is a restroom. It is recommended that every skatepark has a restroom within 100 feet of its perimeter. Agencies that don't initially include a restroom facility at their skatepark quickly find that one is needed. There are several manufacturers of pre-fabricated restroom facilities, which allows for flexibility of cost. It is important to be sure a pre-fabricated restroom is built with quality construction because skatepark restrooms are certain to take abuse. When initially planning for a skatepark, water and sanitary sewer lines need to be considered so that restrooms can be included, whether in the initial development or in a future phase.

Restroom facilities can be designed on site as part of a facility or can be prefabricated as seen by these buildings at Etnies and Upland skateparks.

Site Elements

When designing and selecting site elements and landscape plant material for skateboarding facilities, there are three main functional considerations: traffic-resistance, barrier creation, and directing circulation. Because of the nature of the sport, the aesthetic considerations for skateboarding facilities have some unique possibilities.

Paving

Though the skateable surface of a skatepark is to be very smoothly finished, the outside paving needs to be rough to discourage skating and to provide warning. Parking lot paving should be very rough paving with random stone, stamped concrete, interlocking pavers, or porous concrete to discourage skate boarders from riding into vehicular traffic. In pedestrian areas, where skating is not to occur, exposed aggregate, a heavy broom finish, or plaza top interlocking pavers can help protect pedestrians. This is the paving that can also be used in shopping centers or other places where skateboarding is to be discouraged.

Pine Avenue Park in Carlsbad, California, is a great example of skate-resistant paving. The exposed aggregate concrete discourages skateboarding where it is not to occur.

A very skate-resistant surface, decomposed granite paving at Etnies Skatepark.

These interlocking paving designs at the Spectrum, Woodbury Town Center, and Orchard Hills shopping centers in Irvine, California, are attractive and provide the skateboarding deterrent desired.

Walls

Where walls are to be designed as part of a skateboarding facility or for projects where skateboarding is undesired, there are many innovative solutions that landscape architects have developed in the past decade. For screen walls, where there is potential for graffiti, nothing beats block wall with an anti-graffiti coating. Vines on walls can also be a solution. Stucco would be inappropriate for skatepark design.

For low walls or seat walls, the top of the wall is the most important factor in the design. An easy solution for walls where grinding is unwanted, a rough surface like that of split-faced block can discourage skaters. If masonry is to be used for a cap material, the bricks, blocks, or stone can be spaced so that gaps are created in the cap. Another possibility is to set the cap as a header course with a rowlock brick at 3:1 or 2:1 regular intervals. Most seat walls that discourage skateboarding are poured-in-place formed concrete. These walls can integrate radiused or beveled edges and designs using reveals or joints at regular intervals.

These battered and rough veneered walls act as an implied barrier and deter grinding.

A seat wall outside a skatepark facility with steel edges so the site elements can be integrated as skateable.

This seat wall design at Pine Avenue Park is a proactive approach to redirecting skateboarders away from where they are not desired.

A seat wall with post-construction skateboarding deterrents.

Some innovative planter wall designs with steel edging, reveals, and sloped surfaces.

Fencing

A concern for some owners is the possibility a skatepark can be accessed during non-operation hours. For perimeter and security fencing, it is important to design panels with no horizontal member that can be used as a step in climbing the fence, just standard vertical posts and pickets. A further pro-active fence design approach is to provide pickets with tops having an outward projection or even cane form.

For low fencing, the bigger concern is with top rail design. Both low fencing and handrails need to be designed so that skateboarders are not encouraged to grind or slide on them. This can be done by stepping the rail so there is not a continuous surface to ride. This can also be achieved by providing posts that extend above the top rail. Fencing materials need to be able to withstand abuse, like wrought iron. In most cases, wood would be an unacceptable material for skatepark fencing.

Fencing design is dictated by the level of security required at a facility. These designs show two different levels: modest security with 8' high pickets and high security with 8' speared and curved pickets.

In addition to having a nearby pot as an obstacle, this handrail restricts skateboarders with posts that extend above the rail.

The sloping handrail at this train depot would be a perfect grinding or sliding element for a skateboarder. Adding fencing with a taller and a level top rail deters skaters.

Some post-construction solutions for sloped walls and handrails.

Shade Structures

For skateparks where shade structures are desired, the materials need to be tough. Columns and posts should be concrete, masonry, or steel. Steel and aluminum are the best options for shade canopies. Stucco, wood, and fabric materials would be less likely to withstand the abuse of skateparks. Wood is a possibility for canopies, but will require excessive maintenance.

Site Furnishings

It is important to closely consider the benches and picnic tables for a skate boarding facility project. The options currently available from manufactures are limited. It would benefit the future of skatepark design if landscape architects could design custom concrete site furnishings that could be used by other design professionals. The other option would to be to use steel or wood materials, but maintenance needs to be considered.

A skateboarder is not going use a bench as a skate obstacle if it is unable to support them. These wood benches are attractive and are only going to be used for sitting.

If a proactive approach is not used when selecting site furnishings for the non-skateable area of a skateboarding facility, the result is a need to add post-construction deterrents.

A creative design for a bench, built from recycled skateboards.

A "skateboard rack."

Landscape Planting

Proactive planning using rough paving and other skate deterrents can help the longevity of a skateboarding facility. The use of appropriate plant materials can serve this purpose and, with the correct selection of materials, can improve the visual quality of a project. The best plants for skateboarding facilities are those which can handle heavy abuse either by withstanding it, being able to recover from it quickly, or by deflecting it.

Bougainvillea is a tough plant that provides beautiful color. A Ligustrum hedge is a lush green and can also serve as a barrier. When plants are set in pots, the pots can also act as barriers.

Trees

When selecting trees to be used for a skateboarding facility, the factors to consider are toughness, drought tolerance, low litter, and regeneration. Trees need to be sturdy, with strong limbs, able to withstand skaters' pull-ups. If they can easily re-grow branches without changing the form of the tree, they will do well. It is best to select trees with low leaf litter so they won't present a danger for skateboard wheels. Trees with fruit and excessive or large flowers should be avoided. When specifying trees, high-branching, male trees should be identified. For trees to be directly located in or close to the skateable area, trees should be at least 36" box in size.

Botanical Name	Common Name
Acacia baileyana	Bailey's Acacia
Bambusa sp.	Bamboo
Cassia leptophylla	Gold Medallion Tree
Chaemarops humilis	Mediterranean Fan Palm
Cupaniopsis anacardioides	Carrotwood
Cupressus macrocarpa	Monterey Cypress
Cupressus sempervirens	Italian Cypress
Geijera parvifolia	Australian Willow
Gleditsia 'Shademaster'	Shademaster Locust
Lagerstroemia indica	Crape Myrtle
Melaleuca sp.	Paperbark Tree
Prunus c. 'Krauter's Vesuvius'	Purple Leaf Plum
Rhaphiolepis i. 'Majestic Beauty'	Majestic Beauty Hawthorn
Rhus lancea	African Sumac
Tipuana tipu	Tipu Tree
Tristania conferta	Brisbane Box
Washingtonia robusta	Mexican Fan Palm

Shrubs

For selecting shrubs, one should consider their level of toughness, drought tolerance, ability to regenerate, and whether they have thorns, can act as a hedge, or have other barrier qualities.

Botanical Name	Common Name
Abelia grandiflora	Glossy Abelia
Acacia sp.	Wattle
Agapanthus africanus	Lily-of-the-Nile
Agave americana	Century Plant
Anigozanthos flavidus	Kangaroo Paw
Berberis thumbergii 'atropurpurea'	Purple Barberry
Buxus m. japonica	Japanese Boxwood
Callistemon 'Little John'	Little John Dwarf Callistemon
Carissa macrophylla	Natal Plum
Cistus purpureus	Orchid Rockrose
Cotoneaster sp.	Barberry
Dietes vegeta	Fort-night Lily
Echium fastuosum	Pride of Maderia
Euonymus sp.	NCN
Hemerocallis sp.	Daylily
Heteromeles arbutifolia	Toyon
Ilex vomitoria 'Nana'	Dwarf Yaupon
Juniperus sp.	Juniper
Leptospermum sp.	Tea Tree
Ligustrum japonicum	Wax Leaf Privet
Limonium perezii	Sea Lavender
Mahonia sp.	Oregon Grape
Pennisetum setaceum	Fountain Grass
Pyrocantha sp.	Firethorn
Rhaphiolepis indica	Indian Hawthorn
Rhus sp.	Sumac
Rosa sp.	Rose
Rosmarinus sp.	Rosemary
Salvia sp.	Sage

These colorful planting areas are also thorny barriers. Roses and Bougainvillea are excellent sources for directing skaters where they are to go and where not.

Upland Skatepark has a perimeter of Roses and Mahonia, both plants having pointed leaves or stems. The shrubs at the base of the fencing discourage skaters from climbing when the gates are locked.

Vines and Espaliers

As with shrubs, when selecting vines and espaliers, one should consider their level of toughness, drought tolerance, ability to regenerate, and whether they have thorns. Also to consider are their ability to cling to a vertical surface.

Botanical Name	Common Name
Bougainvillea sp.	Bougainvillea
Calliandra sp.	Pink Powder Puff
Ficus repens	Creeping Fig
Grewia occidentalis	Lavender Starflower
Jasminum polyanthum	Pink Jasmine
Parthenocissus tricuspidata	Boston Ivy
Passiflora sp.	Passion Vine
Rosa sp.	Rose

Groundcovers

When selecting groundcovers, one needs to consider their ability to withstand foot traffic and ability to regenerate.

Botanical Name	Common Name
Acacia redolens	NCN
Carissa 'Green Carpet'	Carpet Carissa
Juniperus horizontalis	Carpet Juniper
Myoporum pacificum	NCN
Pelargonium peltatum	Ivy Geranium
Rosa banksii	White Carpet Rose
Rosa medalliana	Red Medallion Carpet Rose
Rosmarinus prostrates	Prostrate Rosemary
Stipa sp.	Feather Grass

Some tough shrubs at Etnies: Rosemary and Fort-Night-Lily.

Turf as a groundcover is the best regenerative material possible. Combined with Carpet Roses, there is no question of where it is acceptable to walk.

Lighting, Security, and Sound

When designing a facility it is important to keep technology in mind. Too many times athletic facilities are constructed and then the operators realize they would like to add security cameras and sound systems. It is important to at least provide sleeving or conduits so this equipment can be installed at a later date. If competitions are to be held at the facility, provisions for a scoreboard will need to be made. Lighting needs to be fully coordinated during design so that poles do not end up being installed within the skateable area.

Lighting is an important item that needs to be coordinated with the electrical engineer during design. This is the most commonly missed coordination item between disciplines.

When supervision is to be part of operations, planning for lookout areas is needed. The entire skatepark can be viewed from this tower at the China 2008 Olympic facility.

The issue of who should be the skateboarding facility designer has been debated for over fifteen years. Skatepark designers hold that they are the experts because they are almost always former professional skaters themselves and therefore know the details of design. However, landscape architects are formally educated in space planning and construction, so they believe they are the experts. The truth is that neither is truly qualified to design a skatepark on their own. What was once an adversarial relationship is now changing. Rather than competing with each other, these two design perspectives are realizing they need each other if they want to create the highest quality facility. The new generation of skateboarding facility designers is now taking an "integrated team" approach. Companies like ARTIFEX are employing professional skaters, skatepark designers, and landscape architects that have equal responsibility and authority within the firm.

Skate spots are the latest emerging innovation in skateboarding facilities. One of the reasons for this innovation is the result of high-density development and the loss of space for recreation. There have been some other ideas that have come forward as development space disappears and the need for multi-use facilities has grown.

One of these innovations was introduced by the City of Lake Elsinore. After developing a tennis court facility, it was discovered that there was marginal interest in tennis. Rather than remove the facility or let it remain unused, the city removed the tennis nets, purchased modular skate ramps, and set them on the concrete surface. The result was good interest in using the space for skateboarding.

There are other multi-use ideas that have emerged. Manufacturers have developed portable court surfacing and equipment that can be used for basketball and volleyball. These are other sports that can now be interchanged with skateboarding when space or programming time is limited.

This basketball court is a portable facility installed over a concrete slab. Flexible concrete pads like this can also be shared by modular skate ramps.

Synergies with Park Amenities

As new recreation ideas for community facilities like synthetic soccer fields and dog parks are added to the typical public facilities like playgrounds and baseball fields, there are opportunities to proactively design for synergy between amenities. If we consider the community facilities that can have synergy with skateparks, they are playgrounds, roller hockey, restrooms, concessions, picnic areas, amphitheaters, and public trails. Synergistic design should consider this. For family skateparks designed within community parks, playgrounds can be designed in close proximity so that siblings can play in the same general area. When stand-alone skateboarding facilities are designed, this synergy can also be considered so that more stakeholders are served and in more ways.

Lessons Learned

There have been many past mistakes as the skatepark development process moves toward perfection. There have been regrets from users, owners, and designers. If we study these mistakes, we can learn from them to help make good decisions in the future.

The top ten design regrets of stakeholders according to skatepark.org, Skaters for Public Skateparks (February 2008), are:

1. Lack of long-range planning.
2. Choice of a non-controversial site.
3. Retaining of inexperienced builders.
4. Not recognizing the social value of skateparks.
5. Underestimating total facility space requirements.
6. Not considering cleanliness and comfort.
7. Accepting a sales pitch as professional advice.
8. Not understanding that small isn't just for beginners and that big is unsafe.
9. Poor flow and circulation.
10. Insufficient funding.

From owner and designer perspectives, other common missed opportunities are:

1. Including all project capital costs: permits, inspections, and construction management costs in the total project budget.
2. Being sure to account for maintenance & operations costs in budget planning.
3. Hiring an experienced owner's representative to manage the process.
4. Creating a facility that serves the maximum number of residents.
5. Planning for future phase-ability.
6. Providing for multiple users of various skill levels.
7. Including restrooms in the initial construction.
8. Designing for adequate parking.
9. Creating synergies with other facilities like playgrounds.
10. Identifying group use areas.
11. Considering passing lanes, viewing areas, and adequate space between elements.
12. Allowing for adequate queuing areas and platforms.
13. Planning for speed-building lanes.
14. Designing for ultimate build-out so that sleeving and conduits are provided for security, score-keeping, and sound systems.

Chapter 8: *Construction*

Construction of skateboarding facilities can be seen as a three phase process whereby mass grading and utilities comprise the first phase, constructing the skateable surface is the second phase, and site improvements are the third phase.

Depending on the type, size, and existing site for a project, there can be various work tasks and trades required to complete a construction project. The following list includes most of the possible work tasks a skatepark development project will require.

PRE-CONSTRUCTION
- Pre-construction meeting
- Pull permits
- Mobilize
- Submittals and shop drawings
- Demolition
- Clear and grub
- Rough grade
- Parking lot excavation
- Base preparation
- Curb and gutter
- Gross utilities
- Building foundations

CONSTRUCTION OF SKATEABLE AREA
- Excavation
- Base preparation
- Reinforcement
- Setting and welding coping
- Drainage
- Expansion materials
- Forming of bowls and in ground elements
- Building support structure: posts, cross members. Support steel, attaching and leveling coping, fabricating screeds for bowls and radial transitions, transition ladder, 8-Feet radius floats
- Forming and setting of above-ground elements including rails
- Placement of concrete
- Screeding and Finishing of concrete
- Specialty finishing techniques
- Concrete repairs: Filling gaps in concrete, Grinding down concrete, Raising low spots in concrete, Scaling or spalled concrete, Fixing broken ends or edges

CONSTRUCTION OF SITE IMPROVEMENTS
- Site utility lines
- Site lighting and security lines
- Irrigation sleeves
- Building placement/construction
- Utility equipment
- Permanent site element
- Flatwork
- Irrigation mainline
- Tree installation
- Irrigation system
- Landscape planting
- Site furnishings
- Punchlist
- Construction Closeout and Demobilization
- Maintenance and Turnover

Pre-construction meeting

Before the project begins, the owner and contractor schedule a pre-construction meeting with the agency inspectors, subcontractors, and design team. This is basically to put everyone on notice that the project is beginning. It also provides an opportunity to discuss scheduling, inspection procedures, and project roles.

Pull Permits

After a pre-construction meeting, grading and building permits are obtained from the agency building and public works departments. If the design team has done their work, plans have been approved and are waiting for the contractor to obtain sets and a permit card to proceed with work.

Mobilization

Once the contractor has permits, they may proceed to take control of the project site, mobilizing and moving their equipment and materials onto the site.

Submittals and Shop Drawings

In the design phase, there are some custom details that only the contractor can build. Complex items like prefabricated pipes or site furnishings require "shop drawings" that must be submitted to and approved by the design team. If custom fabrication items, like a cradle, need to be built off-site, it is important to have shop drawings approved early to allow ample time for fabrication.

Installing BMPs

Prior to breaking ground, the contractor must insure that pollution is not going to enter the storm sewer system. BMPs or Best Management Practices are devices placed before and maintained during construction to minimize the possibility of storm water pollution. Typical BMPs are straw wattles, straw matting, silt fences, gravel bags, and catch basin filters.

Installation of Best Management Practices (BMPs) protects the site against storm water pollution. Shown here are straw wattles and gravel bags.

Demolition

Once BMPs are in place, the contractor is ready to proceed with demolition of existing site features, if required for the project. During this work, the contractor also identifies the site features to remain, if any, and provides fencing or devices to protect those features in place.

Clear and Grub

To prepare the site for new construction, the vegetation and debris are removed from the property. Ideally, after this the site is reduced to raw land, ready for grading.

Mass Grading

Usually the largest and most expensive construction operation is the mass grading. The contractor performs earthwork and shapes the land by cutting hills, filling valleys, and excavating for bowls, foundations, and other features.

Grading or earthwork is the most expensive construction activity.

Parking Lot Excavation

Unless all parking is off-site, the next construction item is for the contractor to excavate, grade, and compact the subgrade for the parking lot.

Curb and Gutter

The project seems to take shape when the curb and gutter are formed and constructed. These set the boundaries of the parking lot and help visualize the scale of the project.

Parking lot construction with compacted subgrade and curb placement.

Gross utilities

Once the site is graded and compaction is ready, the utility contractor trenches and installs gross utilities. This is basically all the large sewer, water, electrical service, and mainlines. The idea is to have all these major utilities in place so that the site features can now be constructed without interference. When the utilities are installed, the trenches are backfilled and re-compacted.

Building Foundations

For on-site constructed buildings, once gross utilities are in place, building footings are ready for placement. First, the foundation is formed over the utility trenches. When the utility lines are in place, the trenches are filled and compacted so steel reinforcement can be placed and the concrete pad can be poured. The building foundation is typically complete about the same time as site improvements begin installation. For on-site construction, the schedule and process of constructing the rest of the building typically runs tandem with the site improvements.

A pre-fabricated building can be placed anytime after the subgrade is prepared and the utilities are installed. The earlier in the process, the better, so site accessibility doesn't become an issue once site elements begin to get installed.

Excavation

Mass grading would normally begin the removal of soil for large bowls. Once the skateable area is ready for work, the grading contractor excavates for smaller bowls and provides fill and compaction for ramps and elevated areas.

Subgrade Preparation

Wherever concrete is to be placed, the subgrade is compacted, usually to 95%.

Forming of Below-grade Elements

Once the subgrade is ready, the contractor installs wood forms to frame the bowls and in ground elements. A unique technique in skatepark construction is the use of support structures for forming of bowls. To form and work the sides of large bowls, contractors use special scaffolding called cross-members. They also use a convex curved ladder-like board that lays flush with the bowl walls to climb them.

Reinforcement

After all forms are in place, reinforcing steel is installed. Bowls, pipes, ramps, and vertical surfaces will be reinforced with #3 steel rebar. Flat areas may be reinforced with #3 rebar or sometimes with welded wire mesh. To keep the steel at the center of the concrete once it is poured, blocks are provided for the steel to rest upon.

Setting and Welding Coping

One of the specialty items in skatepark construction is coping. Coping usually comes in prefabricated pieces, similar to brick or stone. Since coping is subject to intense abuse, it comes pre-cast with steel inside. For bowls, the coping is placed on the edge of the bowl and welded to the reinforcement cage. This provides stability once the bowl is complete.

Drainage

In most cases, decks and platforms will have a minimum 1% slope so they sheet-flow without need for drains. Where deck drains are needed, they need to be steel to survive. Catch basins will always be needed at the bottom of bowls. The drainlines are typically trenched and installed prior to steel being set, but catch basins are set afterward so they can be set flush with the forms that will dictate finished surface.

Forming and Setting of Above-ground Elements including Rails

While drains are being set, concrete forms are constructed from rough lumber. Though most walkways usually require straight 2x lumber, the curving features of skateparks require bendable ¼" thick lumber with frequent staking. This is the point where prefabricated components are placed with the reinforcement cage and secured to it. Prefabricated boxes, cradles, and rails are placed and tied into the overall structure.

After subgrade preparation, concrete elements are formed and poured. Large elements are constructed first and then flat-work paving.

Forming of skatepark features can require some unusual techniques.

The shell of skatepark bowls encases a skeleton of steel.

This pre-cast cradle top will be set in place on the edge of the bowl and then the two will have their steel tied together. Then the shell for the bowl and the bottom half of the cradle will be poured.

Expansion Materials
The last item to be placed before the concrete is the expansion materials.

Placement of Concrete
Finally, the concrete is ready for installation. As with pools, the vertical surfaces of skatepark bowls and features require "shotcrete," a mixture of sand, water, and cement. This mixture is much easier to work for vertical construction because, since it does not have the aggregate normally used in concrete, shotcrete is lighter weight. This quality of shotcrete keeps it from slumping and it is easier to finish since it is fine textured.

Screeding and Finishing of Concrete
As the shotcrete is pumped into place, a "screed" is used to consolidate the material and to cut it to a consistent thickness by running the screed over the top edges of the forms. On a flat surface, this is known as "leveling." Since skatepark bowls and many walls are radius, the contractor will custom fabricate screeds to create the radii. The industry standard for a skateable radius is 8 feet.

A skatepark facility wall being created with the spraying of shotcrete.

Screeding of a shotcrete bowl wall. The large screed is custom cut with an 8-foot radius.

Floating and troweling of a shotcrete wall. The mixture of sand, water, and cement, with no aggregate, makes for easily malleable finishing.

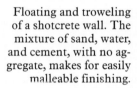

Finishing of a skatepark bowl. A finishing ladder is required to climb the sides of the walls.

Specialty Finishing Techniques

For the most part, skateboarding facility concrete is finished the same as typical flatwork. One of the main differences is the final slickness of the finish. The final smooth trowel does not receive a broomed or retarded finish. Instead, it is very smoothly finished so that the cream forms a slickness when it cures. The slick surface allows the skateboarder to slide, minimizing scrapes and maximizing maneuverability. Another difference with this type of concrete finishing is the used of steel edging. These pieces are installed on the lips and edges of ramp, boxes, banks, and platforms during curing.

Concrete Repairs

Because it is important that the finished surface be very smooth for safety, there are several repairs that may be necessary before a cured concrete facility is ready for skating. The contractor will need to fill gaps in the concrete, grind down rough edges, raise any low spots, correct any scaling or spalling, and fix broken ends or edges. This requires minimal effort and cost, but is very important.

Finishing of a steel lipped spine.

Properly finished concrete has a slick surface. This is performed by smooth troweling to bring the cream to the surface.

Either once the skateable surface is under construction or once it is complete, construction of site improvements continues, with utilities and drainage. The site utility lines are run from the gross utilities so that site electrical, lighting, security, and sound can be installed.

Irrigation Sleeves

An item needing coordination prior to the irrigation subcontractor arriving on site to do the bulk of his work is the installation of irrigation sleeves. This is important so that driveways and walkways do not have to be demolished later, a common coordination error.

Subgrade Preparation

The next step in the process is to have flatwork areas prepared for installation, starting with compacting the subgrade.

A drain line is trenched through a recreation area and covered by aggregate and wrapped in filter fabric.

Compaction of walk-way flatwork areas is usually done with smaller (not heavy) equipment.

After compacting the subgrade, placement and compaction of base material is nex

Parking Lot Base Preparation

For parking lots, paved surfaces require a base layer of compacted aggregate rock. Depending upon accessibility, this may be placed, leveled, and compacted immediately after pouring curb and gutter, or in most cases, it is done after the last heavy equipment accesses the site through the parking lot.

Building Placement/Construction

The building is ready for construction. If it is a prefabricated structure, it is ready to be set in place. If it is to be constructed on site, the contractor begins with constructing the walls. Then he installs doors, windows, electrical, and plumbing. Next, hvac, exterior finishing, and roofing are installed. Counters, fixtures, flooring, and interior finishes are last.

Utility Equipment

Light standards, scoreboards, irrigation controllers, and other equipment are installed in the skatepark at this point in the process.

Irrigation Mainline

While the utility equipment is installed, the landscape contractor begins installation of the irrigation mainline, valves, and control wiring. If coordination has been made with the grading contractor, there will now be sleeves at various paving crossover locations.

Permanent Site Elements

Also set with the utility equipment are any site elements that are to be installed as permanent features. Walls, fencing, and benches to be permanent must be placed at their planned locations and their footings poured. Other permanent features might be bollards, bike racks, drinking fountains, and public art.

Site elements like seat walls are constructed prior to pouring of concrete.

Installation of irrigation mainline with valves and control wires.

Flatwork

Once site elements are located, the contractor continues with site flatwork. Walkways and patios are excavated, compacted, formed, and provided with steel reinforcement. The concrete is then placed.

Tree Installation

Usually while, and sometimes before, the paving is poured, the landscape contractor begins installing trees. This is because once paving has been poured moving heavy trees around the site has the potential to damage the new flatwork.

Irrigation System

Following installation of trees, the irrigation laterals are laid, then the sprinkler heads are installed.

Landscape Planting

Shrubs, vines, and groundcovers are ready to install once the irrigation system is operational.

Site Furnishings

Non-built-in site furnishings are the final site feature to be placed. Trash receptacles, non-permanent picnic tables, and planting pots are placed on site.

Punchlist

At the end of construction the contractor, the design consultants, and sometimes the owner meet onsite to review the construction. The designer notes anything not in conformance with the plans and creates a list of the items for the contractor to complete.

Construction Closeout and Demobilization

Once construction is complete, there are a number of tasks to close the project file. Record documents have to be received, final billing must be complete, and permits are given to the agency. Once this is done, the contractor is ready to remove BMPs and demobilize.

Maintenance and Turnover

Maintenance of a facility usually extends ninety days beyond construction completion. Once plant material has started to grow and has proven to be alive, the owner will request a final walk for a release of maintenance. This is when the project officially ends.

Irrigation installation with installed lateral lines and spray heads.

Chapter 8: Construction

Forming and placement of steel reinforcement for concrete paving.

Shrubs and ground-cover are the last items to be put in the ground.

It is important to start planning for the maintenance and operations of skateboarding facilities long before opening day. Provisions and decisions for insurance, rules and regulations, security, supervision, promotions, and maintenance need to be made to protect the owner and users and to further the success of the facility.

Insurance

Before designing the facility, the risk manager and legal representation need to be consulted. If there are concerns with bowl depths or supervision, it is too late to start talking about these issues when the park opens.

Supervision

There are two approaches to supervision: supervise or do not supervise. Most public agency operators do not supervise their facilities, but most private operators do. At first, one would think the reason public agencies normally choose not to supervise is because of the staffing cost. However, that is not the reason.

Consider the mentality of the liability for CPR training. If an individual knows CPR and sees someone who needs resuscitation, but fails to perform CPR or tries, but is unsuccessful, they are liable. In the same way, public agencies don't want to be liable for accidents on the skateboard facility floor. Public agencies recognize that if, while an employee is supervising a facility, an accident occurs, the agency is liable because they had knowledge of the incident. The irony of this mentality is that if there is no supervision and a skateboarder has an accident, they will not be assisted. In short, this backwards thinking holds that it is better to not know when someone is injured at your facility, because you will be responsible. Public law encourages agencies to protect their financial assets against an insurance claim instead of protecting human beings.

Security

There are basically three forms of security used at skateboarding facilities: physical, supervisory, and open public.

Physical security is used where there is a chance of crime or where a facility is not visually exposed. The frequently used forms of physical security are tall barrier fencing, block walls, and thorny plant material. Wrought iron fencing is the most common. It is important to determine if a physical security system is going to be used prior to development because it is difficult and expensive to install walls and fences after a facility is built. In some post-construction efforts, chain link fencing has been used. Chain link is just not strong enough to withstand the use of a skatepark.

If the skatepark is designed properly, the operator is given a facility that has a security system or at least the infrastructure for a system. Some skateboarding facilities are designed with watchtowers or concessions facilities where staff is able to supervise visually. Others have security cameras to observe operations from off-site or at least from a remote area. This should be considered when developing a facility so that conduits can be installed for electrical and data lines. It is important to know that security can be seen as a form of supervision. If an agency does not wish to have on-site supervision, they are likely not going to want to include security cameras.

The third form of security and the one most commonly used by public skateboarding facilities is open public. This means the skatepark is situated in a very public location, like a major street, near city hall, or adjacent to the police station. Skateparks with this type of security, really don't have security, except when citizens or law enforcement are present. The idea behind this is that the agency assumes no supervision risk or cost, but the skaters will behave under public visibility pressure. If there is a problem, citizens or the police can take action. Though this is the preferred public agency method, it is resented by most skaters because it sends a message that skaters can't be trusted and thus creates a self-fulfilling prophecy.

Instruction

Another operation consideration is instruction. There are many baseball camps and clinics, but not many agencies offer camps for skateboarding. As skateboarding develops as a sport and communities gain greater acceptance, recreation departments need to begin to offer more training and development classes. If a community wants to develop relationships with the skateboarders in their community, offering classes is the way. If children are introduced to skateboarding at a young age through training classes, they will associate skateboarding positively as they grow into teenagers. In addition, if teenagers and young adults are given an opportunity to mentor beginning skaters, they are more likely to take ownership of their community and the sport of skateboarding.

Programming

The uniqueness of the sport of skateboarding presents many opportunities for recreation programming. There are various activities and events that can promote interest in the sport; many also are able to generate revenue. The fact that a skatepark is a condensed facility with a hard surface surrounded by open space makes it ideal for events and planned activities.

For the serious skateboarders, recreation departments and organizations can offer organized sessions so that skaters can interact with their own levels. Advanced skaters can have an opportunity to have the complete park to them without having to watch for the safety of beginners. Another way to get serious skateboarders interested in the facility is to hold professional skateboarding demonstrations. If a community can contact a local professional to make an appearance at an event, the skaters will show. Finally, competitions are always a way to promote skateboarding. If there are local skate shops, they can sponsor the event both financially and by marketing it.

For the recreational skateboarders and families, there are several fun events available. One possibility is sleepovers. By inviting families to bring tents and feeding them dinner and breakfast, the children will become familiar with the facility and parents will see it as a safe place. In addition, movies can be offered. It would be a great opportunity to show skateboarding movies or Extreme Sports videos. Another opportunity for either the athletic or recreational skateboarder is music concerts. The City of Carlsbad holds an annual event where amateur skateboarders and rock bands perform at the same time. A good way to bring everyone together is to hold an Earth Day Clean-up Event. This can serve as an opportunity to not only bring together the skateboarders, but to also use them as a resource for cleaning up the facility, a great way to build ownership. To create income for others, the facility can be used for holding charitable events and for fundraising, another way for building community while promoting skateboarding.

Many of the events will generate some income, but the best programming method for making money is to use the facility for rentals. If the facility has a large group use area, it can be rented for birthday parties, barbeques, and company picnics. Another way to generate some substantial income is through sponsorships. If an owner is able to negotiate sponsorship with Nike, Adidas, DC Shoes, or other sportswear companies by allowing them to place signage or their logo at the facility, some regular revenue can be generated. If vending machines are to be provided, there can be an opportunity to provide refreshments and to collect sponsorship fees from beverage companies. Probably an owner's least popular source for generating programming revenue is through the use of concessions. Most public and private owners are not able to make a small food operation financially feasible because of the licensing, training, and overall operation of a tiny business enterprise. The only successful concessions operations are those run by an outside recreation organization. This would be similar to Little League Baseball operating a snack bar for games. With volunteer staff and a no cost use of the facility, the food operation is a possibility. Other possibilities are for restaurants to sponsor-cater events to promote their product.

Installation of "L" brackets on a curb can deter grinding.

Maintenance

To create a positive image of skateboarding and to maintain safety, it is crucial to have a clean, well-maintained facility. Many people think that skateboarders prefer to have an un-maintained facility, but the reality is they actually recognize the need for cleanliness, for safety, and for the quality of their sport. This is once again an opportunity for skaters to take ownership of their community. There should be consequences for vandalism and littering so that peer pressure can be used. Consequences can be that the facility would have to be closed for a month if it is not properly maintained. This would cause skaters to obey the rules.

If skateboarders are not taking ownership of a facility, it is easy to see. The amount of bottles, cans, and wrappers generated by sodas and snacks at skateparks can create excessive litter. Trash receptacles need to be emptied regularly. If it is possible to have overflow trash and recycling bins, they will certainly get used.

Some skaters bring their own skate obstacles. When skaters lose interest (especially at a beginner facility), they start to think outside of the box to challenge themselves. Schools see benches and cities see large roadway signs disappear, only to reappear as a ramp or street course obstacle in a parking lot. If a skatepark has any loose boards, rocks, signage, tires, or broken fencing, you can be sure that a skateboarder will find a way to use it as a challenging skate obstacle. This can certainly be a safety concern, so it is important to implement a maintenance plan for regular cleanups.

For concrete skateboarding facilities, there is rarely need for repairs. However, if chipping or cracking occurs, it must be repaired immediately. It would be appropriate for one maintenance person to be specially trained and prepared for repairing the skatepark. If this is not possible, it would be wise to have a contractor available for on-call services so that the park doesn't have to be closed while a public contract is being negotiated. A good maintenance inspection plan would be to review the facility quarterly.

Wood and masonite skateparks, as we have already mentioned, are higher maintenance. If your community or business has portable ramps and equipment, there will have to be a staff person available to inspect the equipment regularly. It may be best to implement a maintenance and inspection schedule whereby equipment is reviewed monthly in the first year of use and then weekly after. If any equipment is found to be damaged, it would need to be removed or repaired immediately. One of the benefits of a modular system is the ability to remove components and to be able to replace damaged ones with new.

Vandalism

A skateboarding facility itself is normally not a target of vandalism because it is the designer's responsibility to make the facility vandal-resistant. However, once a facility is in operation, sometimes issues will emerge that could not be resolved in design.

If a facility experiences problems with graffiti, there are a few ways of dealing with the issue. The most common solution is to use an anti-graffiti coating. There are two kinds of this finish: sacrificial and non-sacrificial. When sacrificial is used, it means that the coating absorbs the graffiti and both are removed. The material is then reapplied. The non-sacrificial graffiti coating seals the wall and cannot be removed. It repels the graffiti so it does not stick and can be washed off. The disadvantage of using non-sacrificial is that in order for it to work properly, it has to be a glossy finish, which is generally an unattractive appearance. Another solution to a graffiti problem is to plant vines on the wall. A vine with thorns like Bougainvillea or Pyracantha or with clinging abilities like Boston Ivy or Creeping Fig will deter vandals.

The other most common form of vandalism seen at a skateboarding facility is the damaging of plant material. The best way to prevent this is to install very tough plants. During original installation or when replanting, it does not save money to use small plant material. Trees need to be a minimum of 36" box size to survive. If plants are damaged or killed, they need to be replaced with something tough and large.

Most skateboarding vandalism occurs outside the skatepark, somewhere in the community. It is usually the same form of vandalism, just perpetrated at different places and on different structures. There are now many types of skateboard deterrents for walls, handrails, and site furnishings. If the original installation of a structure did not consider skateboarding, "L" brackets can be installed on edges. Some manufacturers have developed brackets in varying shapes that have a less obtrusive appearance.

If there is undesired skateboarding in a paved area, the easiest and most attractive solution to deter this is to saw-cut and remove strips of the existing paving and then install bands of paving stones. This can be done without even pouring new concrete. Another option is to do the same thing, but to replace the strips with bands for exposed aggregate.

Low walls that are designed with skateboarders in mind are easy targets for grinding.

Chapter 9: Management & Operations

> *Site furnishings without grind-resistant edges make great obstacles for skaters. Post-construction "L" brackets can prevent this.*

Bank: A surface with a slope less than 100%.

Built-ins: Any object or component that is part of the facility and can not be removed without demolition.

Cantilever: an overhanging floor or beam extension beyond the supporting wall or post.

Cast-in-placed concrete: The traditional way of pouring concrete, whereby forms are constructed on-site and the concrete is poured in the forms.

Coping: The round lip that cantilevers over the edge of a pool. This has also become the terminology for the lip at the top of a ramp or obstacle.

Concave: An inward curve.

Convex: An outward curve.

Continuous edge: A long concrete or wood edge with no joints.

Cream: The top ¼" of concrete paving consisting of water and cement that forms a very smooth, hard shell when cured.

Design-build: The development process by which the general contractor has the direct contract with the owner and the design team is under contract to the general contractor.

Drop in: To enter the ramp or obstacle from the ledge or top.

Drop out: A prejudicial term to describe undesirables.

FF&E: Furniture, fixture, and equipment.

Floating: The second part of finishing, where the surface is leveled.

Funbox: A raised flat platform with banked sides and sometimes includes a handrail.

Grindbox: A raised platform for grinding.

Grinding: Scraping one or both axles on a curb, railing, or other surface.

Half pipe: A U-shaped ramp, usually with a flat section in the middle.

Hard costs: The development costs associated with the construction of the facility only.

Hip: The peak on a ramp or obstacle, used for vertical launching.

Jump ramp: A small ramp used to launch jumps.

Ledge: A vertical drop.

Leveling: See floating.

Lip: The top or upper edge of a ramp or obstacle.

Masonite: A wood-based material with laminated layers to make it last long and withstand abuse.

NIMBY: an acronym for "not in my backyard," meaning someone who wouldn't mind having the facility in their community but does not want it to be sited near their property.

Picket: the vertical members of a fence that create the barrier.

Pilaster: a short column,

Precast concrete: a method used to produce concrete structures off site. The structures are then delivered to the site for installation. This is typical for structures needing special testing or finishing.

Prime Consultant: The lead design consultant who is directly contracted with the owner.

Public-private Partnership: A business venture where a public agency, like a city, partners with a private business. This provides a benefit for both parties and also the stakeholders.

Rail: The edge of a skateboard. Also refers to plastic strips attached to the underside of the board. Also a steel obstacle like a handrail or guardrail used for grinding.

Run: A continuous sequence of tricks.

Salad bowl: The simplest form of a bowl, with just one half-sphere.

Screeding: The leveling or creating of consistent thickness by using a screed like a knife to have the concrete pour flush with the top edge of the form.

Shotcrete: The mixture of sand, water, and cement that is used to form pools and bowls. It is similar to concrete, but has no aggregate.

Site development: The area outside the skateable area which is part of the skateboarding facility development including parking, walkways, and viewing areas.

Skateable area: The portion of a skateboarding facility commonly referred to as being the skatepark.

Sliding: A skateboarding trick where the rider slides the under side of their board along the top of a rail.

Soft costs: The intangible cost of development like design, inspection, environmental review, and usually FF&E.

Spall/spalling: A concrete defect where fragments of concrete chip away.

Street skating: Freestyle skating that incorporates all of the elements found in urban and suburban settings. Includes skating on and over steps, curbs, rails benches, etc.

Sub-consultant: A design consultant contracted directly with the prime consultant.

Transition: The curved section connecting two different-sloped surfaces.

Troweling: The initial finishing of concrete to consolidate material and smooth the surface.

Turn-key: A form of design-build development where the owner is immediately ready to occupy a facility when it is complete.

Veneer: the face of a wall.

Vert ramp: A large half-pipe that has 8 foot or higher vertical walls.

Vert Skating: Skating on large custom ramps, half-pipes, and other vertical structures to perform complicated jumps and aerial tricks.

Vert: Basically short for "vertical."

Wall: A vertical surface (100% slope).

A Message From the Author

As a park planner for a developing city in southern California, I experienced the perspectives of users, special interests, legislators, citizens, and designers. Skateboarding is a valuable sport, but with much misinformation. It is unfortunate that a few bad individuals can ruin the opportunities for this sport to be enjoyed by others. The madness our culture has created for competitive sports has caused many kids to be excluded from their peers or to become turned off by sports in general. If this book is able to help one outcast child get involved and enjoy sports through skateboarding, it has served its purpose.

—Scott Bradstreet

Bibliography

Landscape Architecture Magazine

Perry, Robert. *Landscape Plants for Western Regions*. Claremont, California: Land Design Publishing, 1992.

Public Skatepark Development Guide, Skaters For Public Skateparks, Portland, Oregon Skatepark.org

Sunset Publishing Corporation Editorial Staff. *Sunset Western Garden Book*. Menlo Park, California: Sunset Publishing Corporation, 2006.

Wikipedia